GOWER

A GUIDE TO ANCIENT AND HISTORIC MONUMENTS ON THE GOWER PENINSULA

Diane M. Williams MA, PhD

Contents

Series Editor David M. Robinson *BSc, PhD, FSA*
Designed by Icon Design

First Published 1998

© *Cadw: Welsh Historic Monuments (Crown Copyright),*
Crown Building, Cathays Park, Cardiff, CF1 3NQ.

Printed in Great Britain by the White Dove Press

ISBN 1 85760 073 8

GOWI
THE GOWEI

Gower is a land set apart from the rest of south Wales. It is a peninsula heading out into the Bristol Channel owing allegiance to neither east nor west Wales. And yet it is a region of contrasts, boasting much of the topographical diversity of Wales in miniature.

Today, the peninsula welcomes many visitors to its beaches and countryside, as well as to the wealth of ancient remains which scatter its landscape. Indeed, people have always visited Gower, even in times when the rest of the country was ice-bound and inhospitable to travellers. Some have left slight traces of their presence in caves, others have left only a discarded tool to hint of their sojourn here. With time, visitors arrived to stay permanently, clearing woodland and farming the fertile soils for the first time. It is these early communities whose labours are commemorated by the massive stone tombs found on Gower, nowhere better preserved than at Parc le Breos.

But not all visitors have been welcome to stay. For as the number of inhabitants grew, so competition for land increased and Gower became a formal political unit, subject first to Welsh control and later the object of Norman conquest. Historically, both the Welsh district — or *commote* — of Gŵyr and the Norman lordship of Gower extended inland beyond the peninsula. The rivers Llwchwr and Tawe provided natural boundaries to the east and west; to the north lay the foothills of the south Wales coalfield. The Normans concentrated their conquest on the fertile lowlands, located mainly on the peninsula, extending only far enough into border Gower to protect the main east–west thoroughfare. To the north lay Welsh Gower, to the south was English Gower. It was along the line of this route that two castles were constructed, each to protect important river crossings: Swansea on the Tawe and Loughor on the Llwchwr. Both became boroughs, but it was Swansea — as the *caput* or centre of the Norman lordship — that thrived and expanded into a modern city.

Conquest eventually led to more settled times, and the kings of England entrusted the protection and upkeep of the lordship to proven knights and companions-in-arms. By the early fourteenth century, Weobley Castle had been built, not as a military stronghold, but as a fortified manor house.

Although the lordship of Gower remained a political entity, with time, the distinction between English and Welsh landowners became less pronounced. With the rise to power of Harry Tudor and his coronation as King Henry VII (1485–1509), numerous Welshmen received reward for their loyal support during the Wars of the Roses (1455–87). The Mansels were one such Gower family whose social standing rose at an unprecedented rate, enabling Sir Rice Mansel (1487–1559) to begin building the magnificent Tudor mansion at Oxwich.

Gower is very much a region of striking contrasts. At Rhosili, on the western tip of the peninsula, the so-called 'Vile' field system shows a fossilized medieval strip layout. Such a pattern might not have appeared out of place in lowland manors across parts of southern England. Here, the groups of strips retain distinctive names such as Sandyland, Priest Hay and Bramble Bush (Crown Copyright: The Royal Commission on the Ancient and Historical Monuments of Wales).

HISTORIC GOWER

The Norman grip on Gower tightened through the early decades of the twelfth century, with the castle as the principal instrument of conquest and domination. In all, the sites of ten early earthwork castles have been identified within the bounds of the medieval lordship, with the 'ringwork' form by far the most prominent. This reconstruction drawing — based on archaeological excavations in 1960–61 — shows the ringwork known as Castle Tower at Penmaen. The castle was occupied in the twelfth and early thirteenth centuries, with evidence to suggest that the phase I gate-tower was destroyed by fire (Illustration by Terry Ball, 1987).

THE ARRIVAL OF THE NORMANS

By the closing years of the eleventh century, the Welsh *commote* of Gŵyr was politically aligned with the west Wales kingship of Deheubarth. In 1081, the prince of Deheubarth, Rhys ap Tewdwr (d. 1093), had come to terms with William the Conqueror (1066–87) and thus spared the region any serious incursions by Norman invaders. However, the death of Rhys in 1093 signalled the end of this status quo, for *Brut y Tywysogyon* (*Chronicle of the Princes*) records that with his demise 'fell the kingdom of the Britons'.

The Norman king, William Rufus (1087–1100), responded to Rhys's death by dispatching to Deheubarth William fitz Baldwin, his trusted sheriff of Devon. On the command of the king, fitz Baldwin established the castle of Rhydygors, close to Carmarthen. Despite a brief Welsh

insurrection, the *Brut* states that it was from here, in 1095, that 'the French ravaged Gower and Cydweli and Ystrad Tywi'. The Normans thereby made their first recorded appearance in the history of Gower.

But they did not follow up this raid immediately. Rather, early in Henry I's reign (1100–35) control of the area seems to have been entrusted to a Welsh supporter of the Normans, Hywel ap Goronwy. The solution was short-lived. Hywel died in 1106, and then or soon after Henry I apparently gave his friend and ally, Henry de Beaumont, earl of Warwick (d. 1119), permission to undertake the conquest of Gower.

Like all Norman lords, Earl Henry's instrument of conquest was the castle. We know that he built a stronghold for himself at his *caput* of Swansea, for the *Brut* records a Welsh attack on the Norman lord's castle in 1116, sufficient to destroy only the outer defences. From the base at Swansea, the Norman grip on Gower tightened, and conquest was consolidated. In return for military and civil

service loyal followers were granted parcels of land — fees — and with them the right to build their own strongholds. As a result, a string of earth-and-timber fortifications soon appeared along the shores of the peninsula itself.

Nor did Earl Henry neglect the vulnerability of the north-western frontier of his newly established lordship of Gower. By 1116 he had granted the strategically important border Gower fees of Loughor and Llandeilo Talybont to Henry de Viliers. He too, almost certainly, began the construction of earth-and-timber castles, one of which is recorded as having been devastated by the Welsh during the campaign to take Swansea.

These early Norman strongholds would have taken the form of either motte and bailey or ringwork castles. The former comprised a large courtyard (bailey), which was protected by a ditch and earthen rampart, and an artificial mound of earth (motte), surmounted by a wooden tower or keep. A ringwork castle was a simpler type of fortification consisting of a deep ditch or moat and an earthen rampart, entered through a tall timber gatehouse. In both cases the rampart would have been further protected by a timber palisade. It is not known for certain what factors influenced the choice of construction, though both chronological and topographical considerations have been suggested.

The sites of eight ringwork and two motte and bailey castles have been identified on Gower. The remains of the motte and bailey at Llandeilo Talybont are still clearly visible today. That at Swansea was last observed in the early years of the twentieth century, located a little to the north of the present remains. However, some doubt has been expressed as to whether Swansea's early castle ever took the form of a motte. Similar confusion once existed concerning Loughor. Here, excavation has resolved the dilemma and demonstrated that the earliest castle (Period I) was a ringwork in which evidence for a timber kitchen was discovered. The site was probably protected by a timber gatehouse which would also have housed the main residential quarters. This is likely to have stood on the site of the present stone tower. The remains of a timber gatehouse dating from the twelfth century have been excavated at Castle Tower, Penmaen, on the southern coast of the peninsula. Here, too, the building is likely to have provided both the entrance and the main accommodation, as well as supporting a fighting platform.

It is not clear when the first stone fortifications appeared in Gower castles. Of the early earthwork castles, only Loughor, Swansea and Pennard ever seem to have acquired stone defences. In contrast, Oystermouth appears to have been built in stone from a very early date, some time before 1141, when it is known to have been in the possession of Maurice de Londres. Indeed, the castle may have been granted much earlier to his father, William (d. 1131), who is believed to have assisted Earl Henry in the conquest of Gower.

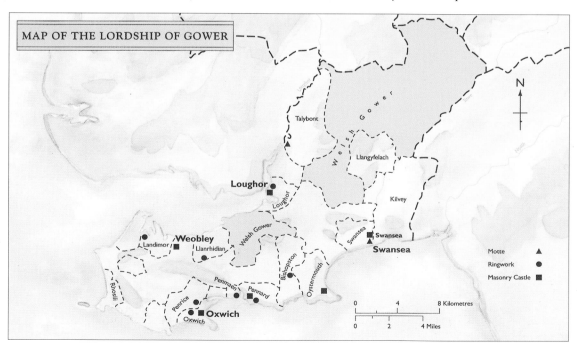

MAP OF THE LORDSHIP OF GOWER

Talybont

Llangyfelach

Loughor

Kilvey

Welsh Gower

Weobley
Landimor
Llanrhidian

Swansea
Swansea

Rhosili

Welsh Gower

Bishopston

Oystermouth

Penmaen
Pennard

Penrice

Oxwich
Oxwich

Motte ▲
Ringwork ●
Masonry Castle ■

0   4   8 Kilometres

0   2   4 Miles

N

The Welsh Chronicle of the Princes (Brut y Tywysogyon) records that in 1151 Maredudd (d. 1155) and Rhys (d. 1197) ap Gruffudd attacked Gower and burnt the castle of Aberllwchwr — Loughor (By courtesy of the National Library of Wales, Peniarth Ms. 20c, f. 163 r).

WELSH REBELLION 1136 AND 1151

Henry de Beaumont died in 1119 leaving the lordship of Gower to pass through a succession of three further Beaumont lords until the death of Earl William of Warwick in 1184. During this time the Welsh inflicted two serious setbacks on the Norman lords of Gower. The first setback came in 1136. Gower was overwhelmed by a general Welsh rebellion following the death of Henry I. The Welsh are said to have killed more than five hundred of their Anglo-Norman opponents at a battle fought somewhere between Loughor and Swansea, perhaps on Mynydd Carn Goch. A sixteenth-century transcription, from the missing cartulary of Neath Abbey, tells us that Gower was then ravaged by the Welsh. This episode must also have terminated Earl Roger of Warwick's tenure of the lordship (1119 to about 1138), for the same text records that Gower was recaptured by Henry de Neuborg, the third lord of Gower (about 1138 until after 1166).

There is no record of castle destruction at this time. Certainly, the *caput* at Swansea must have been safe, for coins were being minted there in King Stephen's name (1135–54) from about 1140. This was despite the overwhelming support for the 'Empress' Matilda (d. 1167) elsewhere in south Wales and the west country. But the ever-present spectre of Welsh insurrection loomed ominously. In 1151 it was made manifest, for we learn from the chronicles that the princes of Deheubarth, Maredudd (d. 1155) and Rhys (d. 1197) ap Gruffudd '... made for Gower; and laid siege to the castle of Aberllwchwr and burned it and ravaged the land'.

We know from the excavations at Loughor that the early timber buildings were destroyed by fire and it may well be that it is this chronicled episode which is recorded in the archaeological evidence. In response to this attack by the Welsh, it seems that the lord of Gower took control of Loughor himself, strengthening the ring-bank and perhaps building the first stone tower on the site of its surviving successor (Period II). By this time, the borough, too, must have been established, for Henry de Neuborg is recorded as granting the church beside the castle, and a burgage plot in the town, to the Knights St John of Jerusalem, around 1156.

Nor was de Neuborg the only Norman invader to invest in his spiritual well-being by such patronage. By 1119, the ancient church at Llangenydd (Llangenneth) had been granted to the Norman abbey of St Taurin of Evereux. Lands at Pwllcynan and Pennard were granted to Neath Abbey on its foundation in 1130 and the church at Oystermouth was granted to St Peter of Gloucester by Maurice de Londres. The manor of Llanmadog was granted to the Knights Templar; and by 1165 the lord of Landimor had granted the churches at Rhosili, Landimor and Llanrhidian to the Knights Hospitallers. Land was also held by the bishops of St Davids at Llandewi and Llangyfelach, and of Llandaff at Bishopston, so that by 1200, significant areas of Gower were under ecclesiastical control. The spiritual arm of the Norman conquest was perhaps hardly less influential than the sword in controlling the lordship.

Silver coinage minted at Swansea in the reign of King Stephen (1135–54) suggests that the caput must have been comparatively secure during the troubled years of the anarchy (By permission of the National Museum & Gallery, Cardiff).

Gower witnessed a period of relative peace during the reign of King Henry II (1154–89), with Rhys ap Gruffudd (d. 1197) appointed 'justice on his behalf in all Deheubarth'. This fourteenth-century effigy in St Davids Cathedral is generally taken to represent the Lord Rhys.

HENRY II AND THE LORD RHYS

The accession of Henry II (1154–89) to the English throne in 1154 heralded a period of relative peace in Gower. The continuing tension between the Welsh kingdom of Deheubarth and the Norman lordships of south Wales was finally brought under control when, in 1171–72, the monarch reached an accord with the influential prince of Deheubarth, Rhys ap Gruffudd — the Lord Rhys (d. 1197). In return for accepting client status to the English Crown, the king appointed Rhys 'justice on his behalf in all Deheubarth' and thereby secured the nominal allegiance of the prince's loyal followers.

Earl William of Warwick (d. 1184) succeeded as lord of Gower some time around 1166 and it was during his tenure that the burgeoning town of Swansea was granted its first charter of privileges. Despite the rare stipulation that burgesses should be liable for military service, the charter is perhaps further testament to less troubled times, reflecting the growth of the lordship's *caput* into a flourishing commercial centre.

Despite the Gower lord's status, Earl William appears to have run up significant debts. By the time of his death in 1184, he owed a rich moneylender, Bruno of London, the sum of £44, for which he had pledged Gower as security. Glamorgan had already passed into Crown custody in the preceding year;

therefore, it was an opportune moment for Henry II to meet Earl William's outstanding debts and thus secure royal tenure of the lordship of Gower.

Just five years later, the strength of the new royal grip was to be severely tested. Henry II died in 1189 leaving the security of his fragile personal ties with Rhys ap Gruffudd in the clumsy hands of his successor, Richard I (1189–99). When the new king failed to act with the necessary diplomacy, Rhys's response was savage, waging war across south-west Wales and plundering Gower.

William II de Londres (d. about 1200) was custodian of Swansea at this time, and in 1192, Rhys besieged him in the castle for ten weeks. It was only when a feudal host arrived from England that the siege was relieved and the castle saved. Although there is no surviving archaeological evidence of this attack, the information concerning it — recorded in both the royal accounts and the Welsh chronicles — demonstrates that it was a significant military action which came close to success. In contrast, there are no such records for Loughor though there is archaeological evidence for the construction of a new stone curtain wall. This was built probably towards the end of the twelfth or beginning of the thirteenth century and involved the destruction of some of the existing internal buildings (Period III). Alas, we do not know whether this activity occurred before the attack on Swansea or in response to it.

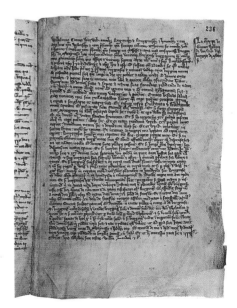

William de Newburgh, earl of Warwick (d. 1184), granted the town of Swansea its first charter of privileges sometime during his tenure of Gower. The charter reflects the growth of the lordship's caput *into a thriving commercial centre (Copyright: Public Record Office, E. 164/1).*

The custody of the lordship of Gower came to King John on his accession to the throne in 1199. He retained it until 1203 when it was granted to William de Braose (d. 1211). John resumed custody in 1208 and continued to hold the lordship in a troubled period through until 1215. This fourteenth-century manuscript illustration depicts the king hunting (By kind permission of the British Library, Cotton Claudius D II, f. 116).

THE STRUGGLE FOR SUPREMACY

By now, John had acceded to the throne (1199–1216) and with it gained custody of Gower. In 1203 he granted it to William de Braose (d. 1211) and thus began the long and turbulent association of this family with the lordship. William, however, was not long to enjoy the privilege, for in 1208 he fell from royal favour, dying in exile in France in 1211. His wife and eldest son, William (d. 1210), were not so fortunate for they were detained at the king's pleasure in Windsor Castle and allowed to die of starvation. Although de Braose left two surviving sons, Giles and Reginald (d. 1228), the family claim to Gower devolved upon his grandson John (d. 1232), the son of William, who had been starved to death by the king.

Between 1208 and 1215, the lordship was again in royal hands. It also came within the range of the ambitions and raids of the native Welsh princes, notably Llywelyn ab Iorwerth (d. 1240), prince of Gwynedd.

Swansea again came under attack. In 1212, it was Rhys Grug (d. 1233) and Maelgwn (d. 1231), sons of the Lord Rhys, who led a force against Gower and put Swansea to flames. Three years later, in 1215, it was the turn of Rhys Grug's nephew, Rhys Ieuanc (d. 1222), to advance into the lordship. This time, the impact was more devastating. The chronicles tell us that 'by the end of three days he gained possession of all the castles of Gower'.

Four are named — Loughor and Talybont which were burned, Swansea, and Oystermouth, where both the castle and town were destroyed. Certainly the destruction of Loughor seems to be confirmed by extensive evidence for burning. Mixed with this debris was broken military equipment which has been identified as debris created by the 1215 campaign.

We know that the town of Swansea was destroyed by the garrison to prevent it from falling into Welsh hands. However, the fortunes of the castle seem less clear. Indeed, we cannot be certain what form the castle took at this time, if it was still in earth-and-timber or whether it had been rebuilt in stone. In 1212, the king's custodian, Fawkes de Breauté, had been paid 20 marks to strengthen the castle, though it seems unlikely that a sum this small would have been sufficient to cover such major reconstruction work.

Clearly, the early or 'old' castle was refortified in stone at some point, for the remains of it were sketched and recorded by Colonel Ll. Morgan in 1913. His plan shows part of an oval, or D-shaped, stone-walled enclosure, straddled by a square tower and surrounded by a ditch. Although these building episodes are undated, we may surmise that they may be similar to those recorded at Loughor. Here, the stone tower and curtain were constructed probably between 1151 and 1215; to posit a more or less contemporary sequence at Swansea does not seem unreasonable.

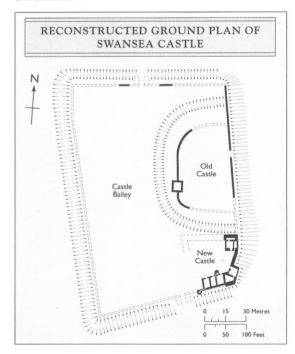

RECONSTRUCTED GROUND PLAN OF SWANSEA CASTLE

N

Old Castle

Castle Bailey

New Castle

0 15 30 Metres

0 50 100 Feet

Beyond the line of Swansea's inner defences lay a large outer bailey. This, too, was eventually defended by a large stone curtain and ditch, though not necessarily built at the same time as the inner defensive works. Whatever state Swansea was in by 1215, the early stronghold appears to have survived until 1217, when Rhys Grug once more swept into Gower and destroyed the castle.

In 1215, Reginald de Braose had been able to secure the lordship through his alliance with Llywelyn ab Iorwerth. However, de Braose collusion with the new king, Henry III (1216–72), led Llywelyn to march on Gower, whereupon the lordship was duly surrendered to the Welsh prince. Llywelyn entrusted it to Rhys Grug, whose savage attack of 1212 must have been still fresh in the memory of Gower inhabitants. Local opposition may have sparked off Rhys's drastic action, for we learn that 'he expelled all the English population that was in that land without hope of their ever coming back again, taking as much as he pleased of their chattels and placing Welshmen to dwell in their lands'.

Welsh domination was to be short lived. By 1220 Llywelyn had forced Rhys to do homage to the English king and surrender Gower. The lordship was at last restored to the de Braose heir, John (d. 1232), son of the William who had been put to death at Windsor. The *Brut* records that in 1221 he repaired the castle of Swansea 'by leave and counsel of Llywelyn ab Iorwerth', by then his father-in-law. The extent and nature of those repairs are not known but they were presumably occasioned by the attack of 1217.

The interior of the castle at Loughor was also repaired following its destruction by fire in 1215 (Period IV). Two ancillary buildings were identified during excavations, suggesting that the main accommodation was still in the stone tower.

The 1741 engraving of Swansea by Samuel and Nathanial Buck appears to show the Norman motte as the tree-covered mound at the centre of two masonry areas. To the north is an apparent stretch of battlemented curtain wall with a square tower forming a corner. To the south is the masonry of the 'new' castle, that area which survives today (By courtesy of the National Library of Wales).

After a campaign in December 1215, Gower fell to the control of Llywelyn ab Iorwerth (d. 1240) who entrusted the keeping of Swansea Castle to Rhys Grug of Deheubarth. This stone head found at Deganwy Castle is thought to represent Prince Llywelyn (By permission of the National Museum & Gallery, Cardiff).

A detailed account of events records that Llywelyn ap Gruffudd (d. 1282) of Gwynedd wrought destruction in the English lands of Gower in 1257. This sixteenth-century manuscript illustration shows Llywelyn at an imaginary parliament with King Edward I (1272–1307) on the left (By gracious permission of Her Majesty the Queen, Royal Library, Wriothesley Ms. quire B).

THE DE BRAOSE LORDS OF GOWER

John de Braose died in 1232, leaving as his heir to the lordship his son William, who was still a minor. Gower thus reverted once more to royal custody for nine years until the de Braose heir came of age in 1241.

The second William de Braose (d. 1290) was to hold Gower for almost fifty years, during which time the lordship was to come under fierce pressure from the Welsh princes of Deheubarth and Gwynedd. First there were border disputes with the Welsh *commote* of Is-Cennen; then, in 1257, the prince of Gwynedd, Llywelyn ap Gruffudd (d. 1282), already at war with the English king, marched southwards into Cydweli, Carnwyllion and Gower. The *Annales Cambriae*, which provide a detailed account of the events of that year, relate that Llywelyn wrought destruction in the English parts of those lands, in particular Swansea, and brought the Welshmen of the area to his obedience. Although support for the Welsh cause was strong in Deheubarth, the conflicting aspirations of its leader, Maredudd ap Rhys Grug (d. 1271), and those of the Gwynedd prince meant that the powerful potential of this alliance never came to full fruition. Indeed, despite Llywelyn's years of supremacy between 1257 and 1277, Gower never seems to have fully succumbed to Welsh control.

A more powerful challenge to the de Braose control of Gower came not from the battlefield but from the court of King Edward I (1272–1307), when in 1278 William Beauchamp, earl of Warwick (d. 1298), claimed the castle of Swansea and the land of Gower. Although the legal proceedings were terminated in favour of de Braose, the case reopened the debate concerning the descent of the lordship. Finally, more than seventy years later, Beauchamp's grandson was to be successful in dispossessing the de Braose descendant.

Meanwhile, de Braose continued to support the English king's cause, and in 1282 Edward I at last succeeded in defeating Llywelyn and 'finally putting down the malice of the Welsh'. In 1284 the king was welcomed by de Braose at his castle of Oystermouth, presumably in preference to Swansea on account of its comfort or security. But this brief peaceful interlude was to be short lived for further Welsh discontent over disputed lands in the north of the lordship was compounded by the invasion of Gower in 1287 by Rhys ap Maredudd (d. 1292), as part of his revolt against English authority. Rhys was joined by Welshmen from Gower and in a surprise attack on Swansea burnt the town and took great spoil before turning his attention to Oystermouth, where he captured the castle. The campaign could not be sustained and Rhys was forced back into Deheubarth by the troops summoned against him.

It was perhaps also in response to the 1287 invasion that the surviving tower at Loughor was inserted into the curtain wall (Period V). If so, it may well have been built by William de Braose shortly before his death in 1290. Alternatively, John Iweyn (d. 1321) who was steward to de Braose's successor, and who was granted the castle in about 1302, may have been responsible. The tower itself consisted of two storeys directly entered from the courtyard. The entrance to the castle ward — which at this time was deliberately cleared of buildings — was through a simple gateway in the curtain wall beside the tower.

There seems little doubt that much of the surviving fabric at Oystermouth Castle is to be attributed to William de Braose II (d. 1290). William ruled Gower in a formative period, and in 1284 he entertained King Edward I at Oystermouth. Three years later, the highly impressive fortress was captured during an uprising led by Rhys ap Maredudd (d. 1292).

The earliest references to the small lordship of Weobley, on the north coast of the peninsula, date from 1306. The castle, which gave its name to the lordship, was raised by the de la Bere family, and was probably begun just a short time before this date.

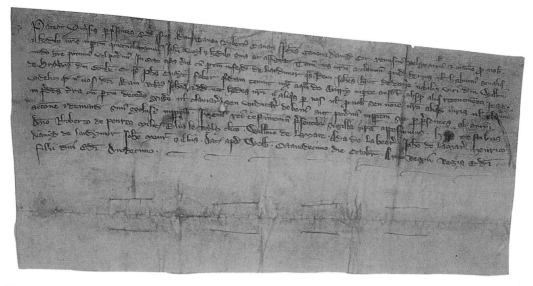

Weobley Castle was certainly in existence by 1318, the year in which this deed was witnessed and signed there by Adam de la Bere (By courtesy of University of Wales Swansea, Grant Francis Ms.).

THE CHARTER OF LIBERTIES OXWICH AND WEOBLEY

William de Braose II was succeeded by his son, another William (d. 1326), in 1290. He too faced opposition, first from the church and then from prominent members of the English community of the lordship, about the extent and nature of his powers as a Marcher lord. A protracted legal dispute persisted between 1300 and 1306 revolving around whether or not Gower and Swansea belonged to the county of Carmarthen and were thus subject to the jurisdiction of its sheriff and bailiffs. By 1306, the proceedings were not looking favourable for de Braose, so, preferring an out-of-court settlement, he came to terms with the men of Swansea and Gower. Two charters dated at Swansea on 24 February 1306 were granted; one to the burgesses of Swansea and the other to the English and Welsh of the English county of Gower.

The charters were mainly concerned with the administration of justice; however, one significant clause referred to the suitors of the action, namely the tenants of the 'ancient knights' fees' which were held by military tenure. These were named as the lords of Pen-rhys, Porteinon, Oxwich, Henllys, Weobley, Scurlage Castle, Reynoldston, Knoylston, Penmaen,

Nicholaston, Stembridge and Forshull, Fernhill and Pilton. This clause is important in not only demonstrating the extent of de Braose's alienation of leading members of the community, but also in affording a record of the lordships of Oxwich and Weobley.

Indeed, this is the earliest reference to the small lordship of Weobley on the north coast of the peninsula and it may be misleading to suggest that its origins had any great antiquity. Just two years earlier, a grant of land at Leason, adjacent to Weobley itself, was made by the powerful Turberville family to David de la Bere, who had been steward to de Braose and one of those named in the recent petitions against the Gower lord. The full and minutely detailed feudal rights conveyed with this grant suggest that it may have been at this time that a separate fee of Weobley was created. It is possible, therefore, that the construction of the castle was not begun until 1304, though it must have been sufficiently advanced by 1306 to give its name to the fee.

Following a protracted legal dispute, in 1306 William de Braose III (d. 1326) issued a charter of liberties to the English and Welsh of his English county (comitatus) of Gower. Weobley appears as one of twelve 'ancient knights' fees' held by military service listed in the charter. The arms of William de Braose appear on this impression of his seal dated 1322–26 (By kind permission of the British Library, Harleian Ch. 56, D. 28).

The horizontal rows of 'toothing' which may be seen in the east curtain wall at Weobley are an indication that the original building scheme at the castle proved too ambitious. The southern half of the proposed range of buildings in this area never rose above ground-floor level.

The only hints of an earlier fortification on the site are the substantial foundations of the south-west tower, which could be compared with the early stone keeps found elsewhere on the peninsula.

A castle was certainly in existence at Weobley by 1318, for in that year a deed witnessed by an Adam de la Bere was sealed there. The castle itself comprises a group of buildings ranged around a small, open courtyard with few indications of serious fortification and no doubt reflects the more settled times during which it was constructed. Most of the building work can be attributed to two, probably contiguous phases of activity, beginning in the early years of the fourteenth century.

The earliest buildings to be constructed were the hall block, the two southern towers and sections of the east curtain. The last-named was intended to form the outer walls of the east range. Surprisingly, this scheme made no immediate provision for the defence of the west side of the castle, or the area between the two southern towers. Although this might suggest peaceful conditions during the time of construction, there can be no doubting the defensibility of certain aspects of the work begun during this first phase. This is evidenced, for example, by the crenellated wall-tops, the watchtower and the completion of the south-west tower to battlement level.

Before the south-east tower was completed, however, the plans for the castle seem to have been radically altered. A second phase of construction probably continued with little or no break from the first: the total lack of defence on the west and south sides would have been motive enough. Evidence can be seen in various parts of the castle to indicate that the initial scheme had proved too ambitious. The 'toothing' on the outside face of the hall shows, for example, that the original intention was to extend the curtain wall westwards. Similarly, in the east curtain wall, 'toothing' again suggests that the southern half of the eastern range never rose above ground-floor level. Nor did the south-east tower.

We do not know the reasons for the changes in plan, nor can we be certain who implemented them. But it does seem likely that most of the work was done during the tenure of David de la Bere (from 1304 to about 1327).

The work completed during the second phase is notable on two accounts. First, it demonstrates a more economical approach to building and, secondly, the work was less defensible. It is interesting to note that nothing was built which was not related to domestic or spiritual needs, perhaps reflecting the changing emphasis of daily life.

To complete the enclosure of the site, and to maximize accommodation as economically as possible, three buildings were constructed: the solar block, the simple gatehouse on the west, and the chapel block on the south, together with a short section of the eastern curtain wall. Chambers were also constructed in the now foreshortened east range, and the octagonal turret was raised to provide latrines for their upper floors.

The origins of Oxwich as an 'ancient knight's fee' are more confused. Certainly, in 1306 Oxwich was held, along with Penrice, by Robert de Penres — another of the named petitioners with grievances against de Braose. Moreover, the Penres family appears to have held Oxwich since about 1237, when it seems to have been passed by marriage from the de la Mares. No earlier references survive. The archaeological evidence is equally unhelpful; apart from the Tudor mansion at Oxwich, which may contain some medieval fabric, there are the ruins of a small, rectangular tower on the headland to the north-east of the present castle. The solid stone walls of this tower have been compared with the twelfth-century masonry keeps found elsewhere as the focus for 'knight's fees' in Glamorgan and Gower. However, this tower never seems to have received any later refortification. If the antiquity of the fee is correctly ascribed then its centre must have shifted and any remains of a late-medieval castle may well have been obliterated or at best preserved in the core of the present Oxwich Castle.

Although the principal remains of the castle date from the sixteenth century, there is some indication that the origins of Oxwich as a 'knight's fee' go back somewhat earlier. The remains of a small, rectangular tower, located in the dense wood off to the left of this aerial view, may represent the medieval stronghold (Skyscan Balloon Photography, for Cadw: Welsh Historic

SWANSEA: 'LE NEWERKE'

It seems probable that by 1300 the outer ward of Swansea was defended by a substantial stone wall and a ditch which appears to have been recut at about this time. We know from later documentary sources that there were north and south gates to the outer bailey, together with a number of towers — 'Donelstour' and the 'tower which was formerly Thomas de Sengleton's'.

It also seems likely that by the end of the thirteenth century, the buildings which today we call Swansea Castle were being constructed in the south-east corner of the outer ward. The upstanding remains of what came to be known as *le Newerke* consist of a north and a south block joined by a short stretch of curtain wall along the east of the site. It is presumed that the enclosure would have been completed with now vanished defences along the northern and western perimeters which would also have included the main gatehouse entrance to the castle.

The south building overlies what is probably the earliest surviving fabric in the castle, and consists of an angled block around the south-east corner of the site. The south wing contains a first-floor hall and service rooms set over transversely vaulted chambers; the east wing houses a solar block set over similarly vaulted rooms. Crowning these buildings is a distinctive arcaded parapet which bears strong resemblance to the adornment at the bishop's palaces of St Davids and Lamphey. This parapet is clearly a later addition and seems likely to owe its inspiration to the work initiated by Henry de Gower, bishop of St Davids (1328–47), at the two Pembrokeshire episcopal palaces.

The north block or north-east tower is a two-storey rectangular building, much altered by later use, but retaining evidence for the north curtain wall and wall-walk of the castle.

The date and origins of *le Newerke* — the third castle to be built at Swansea — are not clear. Architecturally, the two blocks appear to have been constructed between the late thirteenth and early fourteenth centuries, with modifications and additions in the fourteenth century. However, documentary evidence which refers to *le Newerke* has been used to ascribe the building work to the period following the foundation of the hospital of the Blessed David by Henry de Gower, close to the castle in 1332 (now partly preserved in the Cross Keys Inn). Moreover, between 1536 and 1539 when the antiquary,

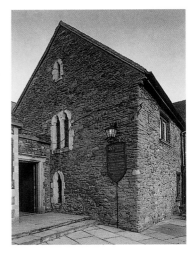

Bishop Henry de Gower founded the hospital of the Blessed St David close to the castle in Swansea in 1332. A fragment of the building, with fourteenth-century cusped window details, survives as the Cross Keys Inn.

John Leland, visited Swansea he wrote:

The olde castel of Swineseye was builded or [r]epairid by the Normans and destroied by Lluelen prince of Wales that maryed King Johns doughter. And it stoode by the bisshop of S. Dauids castel that now is there.

Conversely, no contemporary written records survive which firmly associate Swansea Castle with Henry de Gower, though Bishop Guy de Mone (1397–1407) is recorded as holding an ordination in the castle chapel in 1399, which may point to a more formal relationship between the castle and bishops of St Davids, one that may have had its origins in de Gower's episcopacy. The architectural and documentary evidence are thus at odds with one another and apparently without any means for an entirely satisfactory reconciliation of the two.

We do know that de Braose's daughter, Alina, was married to Thomas Mowbray in the town of Swansea in 1298, presumably at the castle, and that the summons for the Gower lord to attend the court at Carmarthen in 1300 was addressed to his castle of Swansea. This all suggests that whilst the military function of the castle may have declined, the administrative role remained important. That a castle, reduced in size but with an emphasis on domestic comfort, should be built in the corner of the existing castle bailey does not seem inappropriate to the changing circumstances of the lords of Gower.

The distinctive arcaded parapet around the 'new' castle at Swansea is almost certainly to be associated with similar works by Henry de Gower, bishop of St Davids (1328–47), at his episcopal palaces of St Davids and Lamphey. An image of the bishop is depicted on his seal (By kind permission of the Society of Antiquaries).

The de Braose heiress, Alina (d. 1331), was married to Thomas Mowbray in Swansea in 1298. Mowbray's hold on Gower was never secure and was to prove short-lived. Alina herself was imprisoned in the Tower of London following her husband's execution in 1322. The precise provenance of this fourteenth-century carved stone head is not clear, though it may have come from Weobley Castle and is thought to represent Alina de Braose (By kind permission of Swansea Museum).

DE BRAOSE TREACHERY

The last of the de Braose lords is recorded by the St Albans chronicler, Thomas Walsingham (d. 1422), as 'an improvident man who wasted away a rich inheritance by his extravagance'. Certainly, he was called upon to answer to the Crown for the unauthorized disposal of lands in Swansea and Gower, though some of these acts had taken place in the time of his father, William (d. 1390). Perhaps more conclusively damning evidence is provided by his duplicity in disposing of the lordship of Gower.

His only son had died, leaving two daughters, Alina (d. 1331) and Joan, to coinherit his Gower lands. Thomas Mowbray (d. 1322), as the surviving husband of the elder coheiress, Alina, could therefore reasonably have expected to inherit the lordship. Moreover, he had made good his claim by securing from his father-in-law a charter which guaranteed the line of succession in his favour. Meanwhile, presumably due to a shortage of money, de Braose appears to have been making plans to sell the lordship to one of a number of interested parties. By 1319 he was clearly in negotiation with Hugh Despenser the younger (d. 1326), a favoured companion of King Edward II (1307–27) and already lord of Glamorgan. Fearing the loss of his inheritance, Mowbray forcibly took possession of

Gower, only for the lordship to be confiscated by royal intervention the following year.

The Crown's actions were just one of a series of events which precipitated a widespread baronial revolt whereby Mowbray recovered Gower and the hated Despensers were exiled. However, the baronial cause soon weakened and in 1322 the king triumphed at the battle of Boroughbridge, Yorkshire; Mowbray was captured and hanged at York and his wife, Alina, and their son were imprisoned in the Tower of London.

Through a series of contrived and complicated legal transactions Gower reverted to de Braose who, in 1324, promptly granted the lordship to the elder Despenser; he in turn granted it to his son. For two years, Hugh Despenser held Gower together with the lordship of Glamorgan, and thus foreshadowed their eventual unification some two centuries hence. In 1326, an invasion led by his estranged queen and Roger Mortimer forced the king westwards into flight. He stayed first at Caerphilly Castle and then at Neath Abbey from where the court records were sent in advance of his intended arrival at Swansea Castle. More significant was the vast wealth of royal treasure, later valued at over £3,000, which was also dispatched to Swansea. The king fled from Neath and was captured at Llantrisant, without ever reaching Swansea. Likewise the treasure never reached the king and appears to have been appropriated by various Gower families, an act which resulted in several official inquiries instigated by the new king, Edward III (1327–77).

From 1324 until 1326, the lordship of Gower, together with that of Glamorgan, was held by the unscrupulous Hugh Despenser the younger (d. 1326). Despenser is depicted in one of the stained glass panels in the choir clerestory of Tewkesbury Abbey (By kind permission of the Vicar and Churchwardens, Tewkesbury Abbey).

Above: *Henry de Gower's palace at St Davids, its walls crowned with decorative arcaded parapets similar to Swansea Castle.*

Left: *The highly distinctive arcaded parapet added to Swansea Castle in the fourteenth century probably dates to the time of John, Lord Mowbray, as lord of Gower (1331–54). It is a work, however, which bears a close resemblance to designs at Bishop Henry de Gower's palaces of St Davids and Lamphey.*

THE MOWBRAY AND BEAUCHAMP LORDS OF GOWER

In 1331, John, Lord Mowbray (d. 1361), the son of the Mowbray hanged at York, inherited Gower from his mother, Alina (d. 1331). His time as lord of Gower (1331–54) is significant on two accounts: first, although he visited Swansea and Oystermouth, his main residence and land interests were in England, a pattern that would be repeated by future lords of Gower. And secondly, Leland, writing in the middle of the sixteenth century, credits him with rebuilding the 'old castle' at Swansea *and be likelihood Ostermuth also for the defence of the haven'*. This could of course refer to the elaborate embellishment of the castle with the arcaded parapet; it certainly appears to be of about this period if it is correctly compared with de Gower's work at St Davids.

But Leland also tells us that the old castle had been destroyed by Llywelyn, and that this had stood near the castle built by the bishop of St Davids. (p. 16). Therefore, we still cannot reconcile the documentary and architectural evidence with any degree of certainty. It may also have been at about this time that the small stair turret was added to the courtyard side of the south block.

Further claims concerning the descent of the lordship were made by the Beauchamp earls of Warwick. In 1354 the courts found in their favour, only for the judgement to be overturned in 1397 when the lordship again reverted to the Mowbray heir, Thomas, earl of Nottingham (d. 1399), grandson of the dispossessed lord of Gower, John (d. 1361), Lord Mowbray. In return for his services in supporting the Crown, Mowbray was created duke of Norfolk and his family, though rarely resident in the lordship, continued to be involved in Gower politics until 1469.

THE REBELLION OF OWAIN GLYN DŴR AND AFTER

It seems likely that at the height of the rebellion, in 1403–05, Glyn Dŵr controlled most of Gower. His arms appear on this harness decoration found at Harlech Castle (By permission of the National Museum & Gallery, Cardiff).

By 1398, the lordship was in the custody of the king, Richard II (1377–99). In the following year, with the collapse of his power and the accession of a new king, Henry IV (1399–1413), there were fears and rumours of Welsh rebellion. These mutterings were well-founded, for in September 1400 Owain Glyn Dŵr was proclaimed prince of Wales by his supporters who rose in revolt against the oppression of English authority and attacked several towns in the northern march.

However, it was not until a year later that the rebellion threatened south Wales and an attack by Glyn Dŵr and Rhys Gethin of Cwm Llannerch was anticipated. The defence of Gower was entrusted to a prominent Lancastrian official, Sir Hugh Waterton (d. 1409), who made full preparations for repairing and provisioning Swansea Castle against the feared assault. Although the attack did not materialize, detailed records survive in Waterton's accounts for the period September 1400 to September 1402. From these we learn of repairs to the bailey walls and gates as well as the cost of garrisoning the castle in readiness for battle. The relatively low cost of repairs at just 104s. suggests that the castle was in a reasonable state of repair at this time.

There was another alarm in 1402 when Glyn Dŵr was reported to be ravaging and burning near Brecon; then, in 1403, the Welsh rebel turned his attention westwards and took Carmarthen. From here he was able to gather support from Carmarthenshire, Kidwelly, Carnwyllion and Is Cennen. In the same year, the steward of Kidwelly Castle reported overwhelming support for the rebellion in Gower. Glyn Dŵr himself never advanced into Gower, warned away by a prophecy that foretold of his capture if he invaded the lordship. Indeed, although there are records of the 1403 siege of Kidwelly Castle, there are no contemporary records of Swansea being similarly threatened. It was certainly still held by the king's men in 1403 when orders were given to levy supplies in Somerset for provisioning the castle.

It seems likely that at the height of his power (1403–05), Glyn Dŵr controlled most of Gower. Whilst records are scarce, Swansea probably suffered some damage at this time. Likewise, Weobley appears to have been vulnerable to the rebels, for a document of 1410 records that it was destroyed by the Welsh.

Following the outbreak of the Glyn Dŵr rebellion in 1400, it is known that Swansea Castle was repaired and provisioned in anticipation of an attack. The records are scarce, but both Swansea and Weobley may have suffered damage during the height of the rebellion in 1403–05 when much of Gower was in Glyn Dŵr's control. This near-contemporary manuscript illustration shows a violent siege in progress (By kind permission of the British Library, Royal Ms. 14 E IV, f. 281v).

A document of 1410 records that the fortified manor house at Weobley was 'destroyed' by the Welsh in the Glyn Dŵr uprising. Though this was probably an exaggerated claim, some damage was doubtless inflicted, and repairs probably took place. The castle was to be further modified at the turn of the fifteenth century by Sir Rhys ap Thomas (d. 1525). This drawing provides an impression of the castle as it may have appeared about 1500 (Illustration by Terry Ball, 1987).

John de la Bere (d. 1403) may well have met his demise by violent means during the Glyn Dŵr uprising. This record of an inquisition taken in 1410, some years after his death, refers — in the fifth and sixth lines — to Weobley as a 'manerium battellatum', or a fortified manor house (Copyright: Public Record Office, C 137/79).

Although written some years later, the document in question refers to Weobley at the time of the death of John de la Bere (d. 1403), who may well have met his demise through violent means. Weobley is here referred to as *manerium battellatum* — a fortified manor house — presumably because of the lack of formidable defence at the site. It may have been this weakness which occasioned an attack, for the castle almost certainly suffered some damage at this time though it was not completely devastated as the records suggest. It was not abandoned, for just ten years later the guardian of the young de la Bere heir was resident at Weobley when she made her will. Sufficient repairs to make the castle habitable must have taken place between 1410 and 1420, though no works of this period have been identified. The last written record of the castle survives from 1432, when it was in the possession of a John de la Bere (d. 1433), of unknown parentage.

We hear of Swansea Castle again in 1448–49. Two interesting references appear in the accounts submitted to the lord for this year explaining why rent could not be collected for a number of properties in the town. The first refers to 'two and half burgages in the new work formerly held by the master of Saint David's hospital, now in the hands of the lord because the said new castle has been built upon them' and 'One holding next to the castle, formerly Robert Cradock's, which has come into the hands of the lord as the same new castle has been built upon it'.

These references suggest that the new castle or new work was built after 1332, the year in which St David's Hospital was founded. But the buildings which we see today were probably built at least some thirty years earlier, which has led some authorities to suggest that the new castle was built elsewhere and subsequently destroyed, thus accounting for later confusion about the correct identification of '*le Newerke*'. Such an interpretation would explain the dichotomy between the architectural and documentary evidence, if not entirely reconcile it.

A reconstruction of the 'new castle' at Swansea as it may have appeared by the mid-fourteenth century. The illustration shows the building from the south-east. The principal chambers were on the first floor, with the hall in the range to the left and a solar or private chamber in the block seen in the foreground (Illustration by Dale Evans, 1998, from an original reconstruction by courtesy of the Royal Commission on the Ancient and Historical Monuments of Wales).

King Edward IV (d. 1483) granted the lordship of Gower to his most loyal supporter in Wales, William, Lord Herbert (d. 1469). In this manuscript illumination of about 1461–62, Herbert is seen kneeling at the feet of his royal patron (By kind permission of the British Library, Royal Ms. 18 D II, f. 6).

THE RISE OF THE HERBERT FAMILY

By 1462, there was a rising tide of Lancastrian resistance against the new Yorkist king, Edward IV (d. 1483). A number of the Gower local gentry, including Philip Mansel of Oxwich, who was attainted for treason in 1464, did not change their loyalties with those of their marcher lord and continued to support the Lancastrian cause. The Yorkist position in Gower was further weakened by the accession of a minor to the lordship, late in 1461. To reduce his vulnerability, the king placed Gower in the hands of his most prominent supporter in Wales, William, Lord Herbert (d. 1469), the first in a long line of that family who would dominate the lordship of Gower and later the county of Glamorgan.

Herbert was at first simply in possession of Gower, but he soon converted this into ownership by a series of characteristically unscrupulous manoeuvres and was confirmed in his holding by the king in 1469. By now, he had assumed responsibility for all the military operations in Wales against the Lancastrians, becoming chief justice in both north and south Wales, a knight of the Garter and ultimately the earl of Pembroke — and thus the first Welshman to enter the ranks of the English aristocracy.

Although the family's main seat was at Raglan Castle, the Herberts appear to have undertaken some work at Swansea, namely the insertion of the gun ports at the top of the slender round tower in the south block. Similar modifications can be seen at Raglan Castle and no doubt reflect the troubled times during the Wars of the Roses.

Herbert's heir, another William (d. 1491), succeeded to his father's earldom on reaching his majority in 1475. Just four years later, the king removed him from the earldom of Pembroke in exchange for the earldom of Huntingdon. However, events at a national level — the death of Edward IV and accession to the throne by Richard III (1483–85) — meant that he regained the office of chief justice of south Wales in 1483. Although supportive of the Yorkist cause, Earl William was not present at the battle of Bosworth, leaving active military opposition to his younger brother, Sir Walter Herbert (d. 1503). The younger Herbert led part of the forces ostensibly disposed to repel Henry Tudor (later Henry VII) on his landing at Milford Haven in 1485, but he soon changed his allegiance when it became apparent that the Lancastrian pretender would succeed in his ambition to acquire the English throne.

Left: *The gun ports inserted into the upper stage of the round tower at Swansea probably date from the middle years of the fifteenth century, and may reflect the unsettled conditions during the Wars of the Roses (1455–87).*

Below: *The principal Herbert seat in Wales was Raglan, a castle defended with an array of gun ports.*

Following the battle of Bosworth in 1485, Sir Rhys ap Thomas rose to a position of considerable authority under King Henry VII (1485–1509). His principal seat was here at Carew Castle in Pembrokeshire, but he also made considerable modifications to Weobley on Gower. Sir Rhys was also godfather to Rice Mansel of Oxwich.

BOSWORTH AND THE RISE OF THE TUDOR GENTRY

Another influential Welshman also found difficulty in straight away pledging his support for Henry Tudor, and he too was present near the Milford landing in the summer of 1485. Although it was a matter of days before Rhys ap Thomas (1449–1525) met with Henry Tudor, reputedly on Long Mynd, Shropshire, and pledged his allegiance, his reluctance to respond immediately is perhaps indicative of the caution shown by many wealthy families who had much to lose in the event of supporting the losing side.

Rhys ap Thomas was the grandson of the immensely powerful Gruffudd ap Nicholas of Dinefwr who had virtually ruled south-west Wales at the beginning of the Wars of the Roses. He also commanded an armed force which may have numbered as many as 2,000 men. It was this considerable army that he placed at Henry Tudor's disposal on the field at Bosworth and which later chronicles suggest was important in winning the day for the new king. In return for his support, Rhys was knighted and rose in the newly formed Tudor court to hold a position of considerable authority in Wales, eventually being elevated to the Order of the Garter in 1506.

It was to Sir Rhys that Weobley passed, sometime towards the end of the fifteenth century. There is some confusion over how the fee came to the family. It is mentioned in a document of 1472 as being leased to Richard Loughor by Lady Lleucu Bassett,

daughter of Gruffudd ap Nicholas, and it has been assumed that it passed to her brother Thomas, and thence to his son, Sir Rhys.

Although it was to his principal seat at Carew that Sir Rhys devoted much energy and resources, he is credited with making extensive alterations to Weobley. In particular, he is believed to have been responsible for the addition of the porch block to provide a more stately entrance to the hall and private quarters, as befitted his position as a major early Tudor magnate. He may also have made some changes to the solar and chapel blocks of the castle, as well as rebuilding the southern section of the east curtain wall. The traces of a very large late medieval barn which survive in the modern farm buildings to the south of the castle may date from this period too.

Alas, the family's powerful role in south Wales politics was to be short-lived. Sir Rhys's son, Sir Gruffudd (d. 1521), predeceased him, and although he sought influence for his grandson, six years after his own death, Rhys ap Gruffudd (d. 1531) was attainted and executed for treason. Weobley had remained in the possession of Rhys ap Gruffudd's mother, Lady Catherine St John, following the death of her husband Sir Gruffudd, but on her death in 1553, the castle and fee finally reverted to the Crown on account of her son's attainder. By this time, Weobley was leased to a tenant, and remained so until the early part of this century.

THE MANSELS OF OXWICH

In 1487, Sir Rhys ap Thomas stood as godfather to his namesake Rice, or Rhys, Mansel (d. 1559) of Oxwich, or so implies a later report of the christening by a '*Wealsh man who was acquainted with the name of Rice, and such a Wealsh man as was not ashamed of the same name but bore it himself, viz., Sir Rice ap Thomas, who christened the said Rice Mansell at the ffonte*'. The intimacy of this relationship may have been forged through the apparently close friendship of Jenkin Mansel — Rice's father — with Sir Rhys who had invited him to the celebrated Garter festivities at Carew in 1506. Earlier family connections can be traced to Philip Mansel who had fought and suffered for the Lancastrian cause and was married to Mary, daughter of Gruffudd ap Nicholas.

Although the family land holdings had been lost in 1464 when Philip Mansel was attainted for treason, Jenkin's timely support for Henry Tudor in 1485 ensured that the family regained its position.

Just two years later Rice was born on 25 January at Oxwich and so began the story of a remarkable man whose imagination and vigour were to transform the fortunes of the Mansel family.

We do not know what Oxwich Castle was like when Sir Rice was born, for the extant remains date almost entirely from the efforts of his lifetime. Although some earlier masonry exists in the core of the massive east block, it is impossible to reconstruct buildings from this time. Similarly, the remains of the square tower (p. 15), to the north of the site, may still have been in use in 1487 and could be the *castrum de Oxenwych* referred to in a document of 1459.

The buildings which we see today are best described as a mock-fortified manor house. They consist of two independent ranges built around a courtyard, entered through a somewhat pretentious mock-military gateway emblazoned with the arms of Sir Rice Mansel. The gateway and smaller two-storey south range have generally been ascribed to Sir Rice, around 1520–38. The east range was designed and built on an altogether much grander scale with an impressive two-storey hall and an elegant long gallery above. Three tower-like projections to the rear of the

Above: *The plaque above the gateway at Oxwich bears the initials of Sir Rice Mansel, builder of the first phase of the impressive courtyard mansion. The Mansel arms on the central shield are quartered with those of the Scurlage and Penrice families.*

Below: *A cut-away reconstruction of Oxwich Castle from the west, showing the house as it may have appeared towards the end of the sixteenth century (Illustration by Dale Evans, from an original reconstruction by courtesy of the Royal Commission on the Ancient and Historical Monuments of Wales).*

Oxwich Castle was begun by the brilliant and successful Sir Rice Mansel (d. 1559). Although buried in London, this magnificent tomb effigy of Sir Rice rests with those of other members of the Mansel family in St Mary's abbey church at Margam.

building provided very extensive, and almost 'tenement-like' accommodation. These much grander and perhaps over-ambitious works have been attributed to his son, Sir Edward (d. 1595), in about 1559–80.

Certainly, both father and son appear to have been involved in the building of Oxwich. Rice Merrick, writing about 1578, records that Oxwich was built partly by Sir Rice Mansel and was 'latly re-edified or repaired' by his son, Sir Edward. Indeed, it is this account, together with architectural details, which has formed the basis for the accepted building sequence, described above. However, recent debate has raised the possibility that the east range was constructed *before* the south range and thus questions the extent of the works completed by father and son. Perhaps it is more significant to consider how just two generations of the Mansel family were able to contemplate and achieve this magnificent edifice. From fairly minor origins and

largely through Sir Rice's astute enterprise, the family had gained in power, prestige and property under the Tudor monarchs to rise to the increasingly powerful gentry class. Such social elevation was accompanied by a lifestyle modelled on that of earlier feudal magnates which encouraged the development of mock-military mansions such as Oxwich and indeed elsewhere. Sir Rice Mansel also had a life interest in the beautiful manor house of Old Beaupre in the Vale of Glamorgan, where he undertook substantial building work before turning his attention to Margam Abbey.

Despite the promise of even greater power and status, Sir Edward was unable to fulfil his father's visions. Although the family continued to play a major role in Glamorgan society for the next two centuries, their position made no further advance. By 1632, Oxwich was leased out as a residence and the family had repaired to their principal seat at Margam.

SIR RICE MANSEL

As a youngster, Rice was placed into the care of his uncle, Sir Matthew Cradock, whose own naval and mercantile background may well have laid the foundations for the boy's path to fortune. By 1526, Rice had certainly matured, was knighted, and had been twice married. In 1527, Sir Rice married for a third time. His last wife, Cecily Dabridgecourt, had influential contacts with the court in the person of the Princess Mary, daughter of King Henry VIII.

In 1534–35 Mansel distinguished himself in the king's service in Ireland, and was noted for his 'right good exploits'. In 1536 he was made chamberlain of Chester, and a member of the Council of the Marches. Perhaps the most valuable reward for his service was the initial permission to lease, and then to purchase, the site and greater part of the lands of the dissolved abbey of Margam. Over a period of seventeen years, Sir Rice paid out the vast sum of £2,482. As an investment it proved worth the effort, hoisting the Mansel family to new social heights in the

hierarchy of the county gentry. Henceforth, Margam was to become the principal seat of the family. Meanwhile, Sir Rice lost no stomach for the military life. In 1543, as a vice-admiral in command of ten ships, he is reported to have had 'a great fight' when coming into conflict with a French fleet.

On the accession of Queen Mary in 1553, Sir Rice and Lady Cecily became yet more prominent at court. Lady Cecily was granted a place of honour at Mary's coronation, and Sir Rice escorted the queen with a company of 500 men. He gained further honour during Mary's reign, and was appointed to the offices of chamberlain and chancellor of south Wales and the counties of Carmarthenshire and Cardiganshire. In 1557, he was licensed to keep a personal retinue of fifty gentlemen and yeomen.

Rice was now in a position of very great importance, with every expectation of being raised to the peerage. As such, he might have become a rival to the well established

In this grant made by Queen Mary in 1557, Sir Rice Mansel was permitted to keep a personal retinue of fifty gentlemen and yeomen (By courtesy of the National Library of Wales, Penrice and Margam Ms. 1095).

Devereux and Somerset families in south Wales, perhaps even the Herberts. It may have been this Mansel 'threat' which in 1557 occasioned a celebrated 'affray' at Oxwich between Rice's son, Edward Mansel, and Sir George Herbert. The incident resulted in the death of Edward's aunt, Anne, and protracted Star Chamber proceedings.

Just two years later, Sir Rice was dead, and with him died the Mansel family's hopes of achieving still greater fortune and celebrity.

THE CIVIL WAR IN GOWER
1642–48

Gower seems to have escaped relatively unscathed during the Civil War (1642–48) when, along with most of Wales, Glamorgan declared for the Royalist cause. Both Oxwich and Weobley were leased to tenants, and Loughor was already in an advanced state of disrepair in 1587 when Merrick noted 'the ruinous walls of an old castle'. The castle may well have been in decline since its reversion to the lords of Gower on the death of John Iweyn in 1326, for it ceased to feature to any extent in later accounts.

Swansea Castle had continued in use through much of the sixteenth century, principally as a prison, though a town hall seems to have been added to the west side of the courtyard towards the end of the century. Although there are no records of Swansea being besieged or fought over during the Civil War, the town was garrisoned and the Corporation constructed a magazine, presumably in readiness for any fighting that may have taken place. The town appears to have changed sides more than once during the course of the wars, but apparently without serious conflict or damage. By 1647, when Parliament had effectively taken control of the country, orders were issued to slight many castles which, although obsolete, had served as centres for resistance. Swansea Castle was amongst those so named and it seems likely that one of the curtain walls may have been breached at this time. Oystermouth was similarly rendered defenceless.

Gower itself was forfeited by the Royalist marquess of Worcester, Henry Somerset (d. 1646), who had endured a thirteen-week siege at Raglan Castle on behalf of the king before finally surrendering to the Parliamentary forces in August 1646. A year later the lordship was granted to Oliver Cromwell (d. 1658) in reward for his military and political success. In 1650, a survey of the lordship was commissioned which recorded the condition of both castles in Swansea: 'an ancient decayed building called the new castle in the town of Swansea' and 'a piece of ruinous buildings called the old castle'. The distinction is a useful record of the relative condition of the two former strongholds at this time.

Although not a subject of great antiquarian or artistic interest, this drawing of 1831 from the James Wilcox collection is one of a number of surviving early drawings of Oxwich Castle (By courtesy of the National Library of Wales).

LATER HISTORY

The first known illustration of Swansea Castle appeared in 1678 by Francis Place and depicts a glass works in the north-east tower. This marks the first of a number of commercial ventures which were to occupy the castle buildings and precinct right up until the beginning of the twentieth century. Gradually, the area immediately adjacent to the new castle was filled in with both domestic and industrial buildings. These can be clearly seen in the Buck print of 1741 (p. 9) which testifies to the growth of Swansea as a port and industrial centre.

In 1750, the main south block was converted into the town's poor house before being used as a chandler's and then as a drill room for the 1st Glamorgan Artillery Volunteers. A market was erected in the castle courtyard in 1774 and towards the end of the eighteenth century the north-east tower was converted yet again, this time into a debtor's prison and thus became the one part of the castle to resume vestiges of its original function. To this end the upper half of the tower was rebuilt and a double barrel-vault of pale bricks inserted. The prison was operated as a private venture until it was closed through an Act of Parliament in 1858, along with six other similar institutions elsewhere in Britain.

Finally, in 1911, the entire area where the castle buildings still stood was leased for commercial development; a cinema and newspaper offices were built. It was during the 1912 construction work that the discovery of a passage in the north curtain wall of the castle was discovered and fortunately recorded by Colonel Ll. Morgan before its demolition.

In this painting of Swansea in 1792 by John 'Warwick' Smith (1749–1831), the castle is seen surrounded by later buildings of the town (By courtesy of the National Library of Wales).

Without this early piece of archaeological recording work, the line of the north curtain might not have survived. Subsequently, the duke of Beaufort placed the remaining castle buildings in the care of the Office of Works, the newspaper offices were demolished and the surrounding area landscaped.

The castles of Loughor, Oxwich and Weobley have suffered a much less dramatic decline into disuse. Nor have they been the subjects of great antiquarian or artistic interest, featuring rarely in the writings and drawings of eighteenth- and nineteenth-century travellers and artists. Loughor appears to have been in ruins since at least the sixteenth century though the site was later reused when a substantial 'bee-hive' type oven was constructed on the ground floor of the tower some time in the eighteenth century. The site was taken into State care in 1946 when emergency consolidation work was undertaken on the stone tower. The site was more fully explored by archaeological excavations between 1969 and 1973.

Oxwich continued to be leased out as a manor house until the east block fell into disrepair; the south block, however, survived as a tenant farmer's dwelling. This stayed in use as a farmhouse until the 1950s, the eastern end being rebuilt following the collapse of part of the east block probably late in the eighteenth century. The farmhouse continued to be altered and adapted for domestic occupation with new doorways and windows inserted into the Tudor masonry. Two small wings were also added to the west end of the farmhouse, one of which survives on the outside wall. In 1949, Oxwich was rescued from demolition by Lady Apsley and placed into State care, and it has since undergone a lengthy programme of careful conservation and reconstruction.

Weobley, too, came to be used as a farmhouse occupied by tenants. It was purchased from the Crown by Sir William Herbert of Pembroke in 1560 and remained with various branches of the family until 1666 when the castle and manor were sold to Sir Edward Mansel of Margam. A survey at this time records 'that decayed castle called Wibley ... [and] ... barns consisting of five bays adjoining', all leased to William Seys for three lives. When the Mansel line failed in 1750, on the death of Sir Edward's grandson, Bussy Mansel, Weobley along with the Margam estates passed by marriage to the Talbots. In 1911 Miss Emily Charlotte Talbot placed the castle in State care. It has since undergone conservation work, including the removal of the post-medieval farm buildings and the reroofing of the solar block.

A TOUR OF OXWICH CASTLE

The magnificent Tudor mansion created by Sir Rice Mansel and his son, Edward, stands on a headland above the wide sweep of Oxwich Bay. The house is known as Oxwich Castle, and there indeed appears to have been an earlier fortification on the site (p. 15). However, the remains we see today are best regarded as those of a mock-fortified manor house, with clear evidence of sumptuous accommodation, raised during the peaceful and prosperous years of the sixteenth century.

The tour route described here begins outside the gateway, returning to the courtyard and then describing each of the buildings in turn.

The altogether grander east range at Oxwich is thought to have been added by Sir Edward Mansel (d. 1595) about 1559–80. Sir Edward's tomb effigy lies in the abbey church at Margam.

EXTERIOR

You will have passed through the impressive mock-military gateway. It is worth returning to this entrance to appreciate the handsome decorated plaque above the gates. Here, the initials of Sir Rice flank the Mansel coat-of-arms, quartered with those of the Scurlage and Penrice families. A walkway and parapet, set on projecting corbels, surmount the gateway, and were reached via the stairs in the half-round tower to the right. It seems likely that a similar tower would have flanked the left side of the gateway, though any traces of this have long since disappeared.

Once inside the courtyard, the impressive scale of the house is immediately apparent. In front of you looms Sir Edward Mansel's east range, and to the right is his father's earlier and altogether less imposing two-storey building — the south range. These two ranges border the courtyard which is now part cobbled and part grassed over. The original arrangement has been lost; however, the patterned cobblework appears to have originated when the south range was used as a farmhouse. Although the low wall forming the fourth side of the enclosure is modern, it is likely to lie on the line of an earlier curtain.

The courtyard at Oxwich was entered by a showy mock-military gateway, probably raised by Sir Rice Mansel about 1520–38. Above the gate, the impressive plaque bears the family arms flanked by the initials R M.

THE SOUTH RANGE

Turning first to the south range, the two-storey elevation reflects aspects of its occupation as both a Tudor mansion and, later, as a farmhouse. The three rectangular windows at ground-floor level date from the farmhouse period of the block; the smaller two-light window to the right dates from the Tudor period, as does the doorway to its immediate left. At first-floor level, one two-light and three four-light windows survive in their original positions. Although they are partly modern replacements, these windows are all based on the surviving Tudor masonry.

Standing back from the range, it is possible to see a change in the roof line marking the rebuilding of the east (left-hand) end of the block following the collapse of part of the adjoining east range in the eighteenth century. Notice also the 'toothing' on the east range at this point which suggests that originally there may have been plans to raise the south range to three storeys.

The doorway in the curtain wall to the right of the south range allows access to wall-walk level via a stone spiral stair.

The south range is entered through a doorway which, in its present form, dates from the farmhouse period. The porch

Sir Rice Mansel's south range at Oxwich Castle.

dressings make use of Tudor stonework, pillaged from elsewhere in the castle. The room which you enter (the modern ticket point) was probably the sixteenth-century kitchen, on account of its size and position beneath the great chamber at first-floor level. The room still retains its original fireplace and a small brick-built oven, which was set into the far wall (beneath the timber stairs), and perhaps dates from the later alterations to this end of the building.

To the right, adjacent to the kitchen, is a middle room which also retains its original fireplace. This chamber now houses an exhibition. Beyond, two doorways lead into what were two inner rooms, though their dividing partition is no longer present. Together, the middle and inner rooms (now rerendered) were probably service rooms, occupied in the main by the family's servants.

The first floor is reached via a modern staircase at the kitchen end of the range. This upper storey was divided into two rooms which are presently occupied by an exhibition. Although these chambers are now open to the roof, they would have had ceilings and an attic level above. At the top of the stairs, further evidence of the rebuilding operation which took place following the collapse of the east range, can be seen in the window opening on your left. This room was heated by a fireplace which still retains its original jambs though the lintel above is a more recent insertion.

A lath and plaster screen separates the two rooms. This partition dates from about 1600–50, but is likely to have replaced an earlier screen. Parts of it have been left unfinished so that it is possible to appreciate the various stages of construction.

1 Gateway — *A pretentious mock-military entrance intended more for show than for serious defence. The plaque above the gate bears the arms of the Mansel family.*

2 Newel Stair — *A small projecting tower contained a stair giving access to the upper levels from both the courtyard and the first floor of the south range.*

3 Courtyard — *Now partly cobbled and partly grassed over, this area may well have been adorned with garden features in the Tudor period.*

4 South Range — *The earliest part of the house, thought to have been built by Sir Rice Mansel about 1520–38.*

A BIRD'S-EYE VIEW OF OXWICH CASTLE
FROM THE WEST

(Illustration by John Banbury)

5 Upper Floor of South Range — *The two chambers at this level provided the principal accommodation in the early Tudor house, namely a great chamber and a private bedroom.*

6 Site of Porch — *Foundations mark the position of a projecting stone porch which contained a staircase leading to the first floor of the east range.*

7 East Range — *The construction of this highly ambitious block of chambers, with its three projecting towers, may well have bankrupted Sir Edward Mansel. It was probably raised about 1559–80.*

8 Hall — *Two large blocked windows at this level lit an imposing hall within the east range.*

9 Long Gallery — *The remains of four windows in the west face of the east range, together with a single large opening in the gable of the southern end, provide evidence of a handsome long gallery at the top of the building.*

10 Pillar Stair — *Two pillar staircases, one at either end of the building, led to the various upper levels of the east range. The better preserved is found in a corner at the southern end, and allowed access to the hall and to the accommodation in the nearby south-east tower.*

11 South-East Tower — *This six-storey structure still survives to its full height, with each floor retaining evidence of comparatively comfortable accommodation.*

12 North-East Tower — *This is not as well preserved as the south-east tower. It is suggested that the earliest masonry at the site may lie in the lower courses of the east range near this point.*

13 Dovecot — *By the Tudor period, such structures were possibly as much symbols of status as ones of practical necessity. The Oxwich dovecot may have housed up to 300 nests, with doves and pigeons a year-round source of fresh meat.*

The second chamber also retains the jamb elements of its original fireplace, and like its counterpart in the adjoining room, has since been modified. In the far corner of the room is a doorway to the spiral stair which led directly from the courtyard, and on up to the attic level. A second door, directly above the first, allowed access to the roof space which was lit by a small, two-light window in the gable-end wall. Access could also be gained to the wall-walk above the gateway via the spiral stair.

The two first-floor chambers would have formed the principal accommodation in the early Tudor house, namely the great chamber and a bedroom. At one time furnished with wall hangings and items displaying the Mansels' wealth, these rooms would have offered great comfort compared with their medieval counterparts, as befitted the family's position of increasing influence in the burgeoning gentry class.

THE EAST RANGE

Returning to the courtyard, and looking at the east range, you are faced with numerous window openings and doorways — some still open and some which have been blocked. Although it is now difficult to appreciate fully the original design of the building, it is possible to unravel at least some of its arrangements.

The elevation at which you are looking traverses gently steepening ground from left to right, with the result that to your left the building is at least five storeys high, and to your right, just four. To the right of the dressed stone doorway at ground level, there is a vaulted basement, over which the first-floor hall rose two storeys high, and was itself surmounted by a long gallery. Above the same doorway, and to its left, there appear to have been at least four separate floor levels below the long gallery which extended the entire length of the range.

At ground level, in addition to the dressed stone doorway described above, there is a second entrance to your right, adjacent to the south block. At first-floor

A general view of Oxwich Castle from the west. The two ranges — south to the right and east to the left — appear to have been designed independently, each capable of serving a discrete household.

light openings, and presumably lit the dais end of the hall.

To the left of the doorway into the hall there are the remains of a square-headed two-light window which lit a room above the passage below. Two similar windows, two floors above, are also visible, as are a number of further openings which are all now blocked. Evidence for the long gallery at the top of the building is provided by the remains of four windows which would have provided a flood of light, as well as fine views of the surrounding countryside.

Continue through the small doorway adjacent to the south range, and you enter a part of the site that collapsed sometime in the eighteenth century. Looking towards the gable end of the building, to the right you will see the remains of a pillar stair which gave access to the accommodation adjacent to the hall, and in the nearby south-east tower. It is probably one of the earliest examples of this type of stair in the locality and consists of a series of straight flights arranged around a solid masonry core.

To the left of the stair, the accommodation arrangements for the rooms to the south of the hall can be identified in the surviving elevation. There were four floors, the lower two of which were lit by two single-light windows containing window seats. The room above appears to have been more lavishly furnished, with a fireplace, and with two tall windows, each of two paired lights with seats. This may have been a principal family room. The topmost floor contains the gable-end window of the long gallery.

level, a large blocked doorway is visible. This was the principal entrance to the range and was approached via a stairway in a projecting porch from the courtyard. Only the foundations of this porch now survive at courtyard level. To its right are the remains of two massive windows, both of which are now blocked. These lit the hall which occupied both the first and second floors at this end of the building. The best-surviving window comprises three bays, each of which has three tiers of two-light windows (eighteen openings in all). To its right, only the southernmost jamb of the second window survives. This is of similar design to its companion, but consisted of four tiers of two-

SOUTH-EAST TOWER

From the rooms at the south end of the east range, doorways lead into the south-east tower — one of three multi-storey projections which extended from the rear of the east range. It still survives to six storeys, and would have provided extensive accommodation. Each floor was well provided with windows, and there is a fireplace at all levels except the ground floor. Although comfortable, the chambers were in no way comparable with those just observed adjoining the hall. It may well be that these rooms were reserved for the many gentlemen retainers Sir Rice, and perhaps Sir Edward too, were authorized to house (p. 27).

The south-east tower was one of three multi-storey projections extending from the east range at Oxwich. It may have been intended to house gentlemen retainers of the household.

THE OXWICH BROOCH

The fourteenth-century Oxwich Brooch was originally designed with three rubies and three cameos in elaborate gold settings (By permission of the National Museum & Gallery, Cardiff).

In 1968, through great good fortune, a precious and most exciting object was found during clearance and conservation work at the castle. Since known as the Oxwich Brooch, the gold ring-brooch with its jewel settings is one of the finest surviving pieces of medieval jewellery from anywhere in Britain.

The brooch itself is just two inches (44mm) in diameter and originally held three rubies (only two remain) and three cameos in six elaborate gold settings. A close analysis of the construction of the brooch has revealed that whilst the gold setting was made between 1320 and 1340, the portraiture depicted on the cameos suggests a date of manufacture sometime in the thirteenth century, perhaps as much as seventy years earlier. The brooch must therefore have been repaired at some time and the lost rubies replaced with three ill-fitting cameos, possibly rescued from an earlier piece of jewellery.

Clearly, the brooch was of great value as well as antiquity. Its discovery in a sixteenth-century building at Oxwich raises the question of how it came to be in Mansel ownership. It may simply have been a gift from the Tudor court or it may have been a family heirloom spirited away from a much earlier royal treasure. For in 1326, on his flight from his estranged wife, Edward II spent some time in south Wales, staying first at Caerphilly and then at Neath. He travelled with his court and a very considerable royal treasure, at least some of which was dispersed at Swansea, following his abdication, and never recovered by the Crown. Despite over ten years of commissions of inquiry, with heavy suspicion laid on Gower men, including Robert de Penres, who held Oxwich at this time, the whereabouts of this treasure remained unknown. Perhaps the Oxwich brooch was part of this prized royal hoard, handed down to succeeding generations, only to be lost again for centuries until chance recovery in the twentieth century. The brooch can now be seen on display at the National Museum & Gallery in Cardiff.

It is worth looking at the exterior of this remarkable structure and considering each elevation in turn. Despite its apparent uniformity, there are a number of variations in the window arrangements between each floor and between each face. Whether these differences are related to status, function or simply to building peculiarities is not known.

Nearby, the middle tower survives only as foundations. Again, it is not known whether this tower offered tenement-like accommodation or indeed, if it was ever raised beyond more than one or two levels.

HALL AND BASEMENT

Something of the hall arrangements have already been described from the courtyard façade. The rear of this elevation demonstrates more clearly the two-storey nature of the hall as well as the exact position of the two massive windows described earlier. The hall itself is set above a spacious basement which can be reached by way of the modern timber stairs.

Two large barrel-vaulted undercrofts supported the hall structure and would have offered extensive storage facilities for the large number of occupants of the castle. Close to where you enter the first of the basement chambers are the remains of a newel stair which provided direct access into the central tower. This room was lit by a single window opening on to the courtyard, an arrangement mirrored in the adjoining chamber, though this was also served by a second window in the opposite wall. A narrow mural stair in the second chamber provided access to a passage at the north end of the hall.

NORTH-EAST TOWER

Leaving the basement by the wide doorway at its northern end, you enter a passage and directly opposite you is a second, though less well-preserved, pillar stair which provided access to the rooms to the left and to those located in the north-east tower to the right. It is in this area that some of the earliest masonry in the castle has been identified, perhaps dating from the later medieval structure which is recorded as belonging to Philip Mansel in 1459.

Turn right and continue into the basement level of the north-east tower where the remains of an oven are visible, suggesting that this was once a kitchen. From here, the rear of the courtyard elevation demonstrates the complexity of the floor and room arrangements at this end of the building. Once more, it is difficult to provide a precise explanation of the exact scheme, though it is clear that additional floors were inserted above and to the right of the passage. Moreover, the intention may have been to extend into the courtyard and thus create a northern wing in place of the flimsy curtain which apparently existed at this time. Such a plan would have been in keeping with similar buildings raised at this time, such as Old Beaupre Castle in the Vale of Glamorgan, in which Sir Rice held a life interest from 1516.

DOVECOT

Outside the enclosed courtyard area are the substantial remains of a dovecot, probably erected during the first Tudor building episode at Oxwich. One side has collapsed, and it has lost its corbelled stone roof. Originally, the dovecot would have housed some 300 nests arranged in eleven tiers. It was entered through a small door located on the east side. The primary purpose for keeping doves and pigeons was to provide a year-round supply of fresh meat. But it was a privilege restricted to those of some rank in medieval times and thus dovecots became a symbol of status. Although the practice of building such structures was gradually extending to lower social ranks by the time of Sir Rice Mansel, the medieval form of the Oxwich dovecot may have been a deliberate attempt to give credence to the supposedly ancient origins of the family.

A symbol of status as much as practical need, the dovecot at Oxwich would probably have housed up to 300 nests.

A TOUR OF
WEOBLEY CASTLE

Weobley is particularly memorable for its dramatic location, perched on the northern windswept coast of the Gower peninsula. It overlooks the wide sweep of Llanrhidian marsh with the Llwchwr estuary beyond. But for all its apparent desolation, the buildings at Weobley reveal an emphasis upon gracious living and domestic comfort, with defensive measures apparently of secondary consideration.

The buildings which stand today were raised principally by the de la Bere family in two successive phases between 1304 and 1327. The substantial remains of four ranges survive: surrounding a small courtyard, they give a deceptive impression of impregnability which belies the comparative luxury afforded by this *manerium batellatum*, or fortified manor house (see p. 21).

The tour route described here begins outside the main gateway to the castle. Each of the buildings is described in turn, beginning with those in the southern range and moving anti-clockwise to return eventually to the gateway. However, as you approach the castle, on your right you will pass the modern farmyard which is bounded on one side (south) by the substantial remains of a large, late medieval barn, built perhaps for Sir Rhys ap Thomas (p. 24).

EXTERIOR

Before entering the castle, it is worth pausing on the flat grassed area in front of the gateway to study the external features of the building. The castle is constructed mainly of rubble masonry of local origin with dressings around windows and doors principally of Old Red Sandstone, yellow sandstone and, occasionally, Sutton stone from quarries near Ogmore in the Vale of Glamorgan. Limekilns on the site (p. 42) suggest that local outcrops of Carboniferous limestone were exploited to make mortar.

Although deceptively strong, the defensibility of the gateway is minimal. The shallow rock-cut ditch along this flank provided no serious defence and may have been more use as a source of limestone for the mortar. To the left, the gateway is flanked by the solar and to the right, by the cistern turret of the south-west tower.

Left: The buildings at Weobley Castle were raised in two principal phases by the de la Bere family during the fourteenth century. This seal of John de la Bere (d. 1388) is dated to 1341 and bears a much worn impression of the family coat-of-arms (By courtesy of the National Library of Wales, Penrice and Margam collection, ref. 2804, 4).

Right: Weobley Castle occupies a dramatic position overlooking the wide Llanrhidian marsh (Skyscan Balloon Photography, for Cadw: Welsh Historic Monuments).

Despite the fact that the solar range and gateway were crowned by a crenellated parapet, arrowloops do not exist below this level, thus limiting the defensive possibilities of the main façade of the castle.

To the left, beyond the solar block, 'toothing' on the outer wall of the hall can be seen, indicating that the original plan was to extend this wall further west.

THE GATEWAY

The castle is entered through a simple gateway. The arch is high enough for a mounted rider to pass through, and was closed with large wooden doors, but there was no portcullis. Around the entrance itself, stone toothing indicates some sort of projecting building or buttresses, though the lack of any substantial remains suggests that the structure may have been quite flimsy.

The gateway was an exceptionally long building and served a dual purpose. Along with the solar, which was built at the same time, it closed the vulnerable west front of the castle between the hall and south-west tower. In addition, the room over the gate-passage would have provided a large domestic chamber with access into the solar and perhaps into the south-west tower too, though no evidence of this survives. The red sandstone corbels which would have carried the timber floor of the upper room can still be seen. At ground level, however, the gateway initially awkwardly abutted the corner of the earlier south-west tower; that is until the cistern turret was built to mask this clumsy junction during the second phase of the initial building period.

A second, open archway, directly opposite the first, gives access to the courtyard around which the buildings are grouped. All of the main rooms were situated at first-floor level.

1 Gateway — *The castle was entered through a simple gate high enough for a mounted rider to pass through and closed by large wooden doors; but there was no portcullis.*

2 Masonry Toothing — *The projecting rows of masonry against the north-west corner of the solar and on the south face of the east range indicate a more ambitious design for the castle. Walls meant to join up with these areas were never built.*

3 Chamber over Gateway — *The room over the gate-passage provided additional domestic accommodation.*

The simple gateway at Weobley closed off the vulnerable west front of the castle, with its upper room providing an additional domestic chamber.

(Illustration by John Banbury)

4 South-West Tower — *Originally freestanding, the walls in this tower are much thicker than elsewhere in the castle. It may be the earliest masonry feature on the site.*

5 Cistern Turret — *This turret is so named because the pit at its lowest level may have been a cistern to store rain water channelled from the roofs.*

6 Chapel Block — *A two-storey structure erected in the second phase of fourteenth-century building, with the chapel thought to have been located at the upper level.*

7 South-East Tower — *Intended as a strong defensible structure, with at least three upper levels, it was probably never completed.*

8 Limekiln — *One corner of the south-east tower was built over a limekiln, probably used for the production of mortar during the building work.*

9 East Range — *The southern end of this range may never have been raised above foundation level. The northern half was originally of two storeys and may have been planned with a guest chamber set over a servants' hall.*

10 Latrine Turret — *This polygonal turret housed latrines to serve three levels in the adjacent wing.*

11 Porch — *Added about 1500, it provided a more fitting and imposing entrance to the hall.*

12 Hall and Kitchen — *The ground floor in this large block probably served as the kitchen. The hall was on the upper floor.*

13 Solar — *A private withdrawing chamber for the lord and his family. A passage leading from the solar gave access to a latrine and also to the room over the gateway.*

THE SOUTH-WEST TOWER AND CISTERN TURRET

Once inside the courtyard, to the right you will find the remains of the south-west tower — perhaps the earliest building at Weobley. Originally freestanding, the massive walls are thicker than anywhere else in the castle. The tower may have had two floors above the basement. Although no traces now remain, this would have been entered from the courtyard at first-floor level, via an external flight of stone or timber stairs.

The defensive capabilities of this tower would have been severely reduced by the construction of the adjacent chapel block and the cistern turret, since it would no longer have projected beyond the curtain wall as originally planned.

The cistern turret is so named because of the pit contained within its lowermost level which has been interpreted as a cistern to store rain water channelled from the adjoining roofs. Noticeably, there is no other provision for water storage at Weobley, nor has a well been identified.

This finely worked early fourteenth-century stonework is thought to derive from a piscina *within the castle chapel at Weobley (By courtesy of the Royal Commission on the Ancient and Historical Monuments of Wales).*

THE CHAPEL BLOCK

Adjacent to the south-west tower is the so-called chapel block. This two-storey building was erected in the second phase of the fourteenth-century building operation to complete the replanned south-east corner of the enclosure.

The presumed location of a chapel at first-floor level is based on the recovery, during excavations, of what has been interpreted as the finely worked head of a *piscina* — a small sink used for washing sacramental vessels. The chapel was probably entered directly from the courtyard via an external timber staircase.

The ground-floor room contained a window and was connected to the courtyard by doorways at either end of the building, and a postern door pierced the outer wall.

Traces of later, probably fifteenth-century building activity abut both sides of the chapel block and have been interpreted as the sub-structures for side chambers flanking the chapel above.

THE SOUTH-EAST TOWER

Back inside the courtyard, a second postern doorway on the east side gives access to the unfinished southern end of the east range, and to the substantial foundations of the south-east tower beyond.

The south-east tower was intended to have been a strong defensible structure with at least three upper levels, rivalled in size only by the south-west tower. Square in plan, the outer corners of the tower rose as semi-pyramidal spurs to the few remaining lower courses which show the intended polygonal form of the structure.

Three separate latrine chutes discharge into a vaulted passage running beneath the inner side of the tower, providing unequivocal evidence of the early intention to raise the building to at least a similar number of floors. The reasons for the drastic reduction in the initial building scheme are not known; however, it seems likely that economic as well as military considerations may have been responsible (p. 14).

One corner of the tower rests on a circular limekiln, used for the production of mortar during building work.

A view across the chapel block to the south-west tower and gateway at Weobley.

One corner of Weobley's proposed south-east tower rests on a circular limekiln.

EASTERN RANGE

It is as well to consider the range of buildings on the east side of the courtyard in two sections.

Beginning at the southern end, it seems that this area — like the south-east tower — was never raised above foundation level. It clearly presented a weak front to the castle, for the curtain wall in this area was completely reconstructed in the fifteenth century, perhaps as a result of destruction by military action during the Glyn Dŵr uprising (pp. 20–21).

The only clues to the planned arrangement can be found in features originally intended to enhance the rooms in the range, but now displayed on the exterior of the shrunken curtain walls. A ground-level fireplace and a first-floor door in the northern wall of this unit demonstrate the intention to integrate the two halves of the eastern range, with a continuous curtain raised along its perimeter. The toothing to receive this southern extension to the curtain wall is still visible on the projecting stub of the eastern curtain wall.

Had it been completed, the southern end of the range would probably have provided additional domestic accommodation on two levels, similar to that which can be seen in the adjacent northern section. An oven and fireplace, tucked into the wall behind the south-east tower, together with a drain running out through the base of a small projecting turret to the north of the tower, suggest that the basement was intended to serve as a kitchen or bakehouse.

Other foundations in this area are thought to represent later, post-medieval building work.

You should now return back into the courtyard where, in the far corner, a modern pointed-arched doorway leads into the basement of the hall block. From here, cross the paved floor, and continue through the earth-floored passage to the northern part of the east range.

The external walls were raised in the first building campaign, and it was not until the second phase, admittedly without an appreciable break in the work, that the internal walls and the north-east turret were added.

When completed, this range connected with the hall block at its upper and lower levels by way of the storeyed passage through which you have just walked. This was built against the north-east curtain wall, and provided access to latrines which can be seen in the external projection on the curtain wall.

Initially, the range had two storeys and may have been conceived with guest accommodation at first-floor level, and a servants' hall below, though later alterations make it difficult to determine the original arrangements precisely. By the late fifteenth century, the upper floor level had been lowered and another floor inserted above. Subsequent alterations to the porch building in the sixteenth century obliterated evidence for

The porch fronting the north range at Weobley was added about 1500 by Sir Rhys ap Thomas.

the building sequence still further, and suggest that by this time, the east range was deserted.

Despite this complicated sequence of sub-division of the rooms, each chamber always appears to have been provided with a fireplace, windows and discrete access to a latrine, demonstrating that this suite was designed with comfort and convenience as the uppermost considerations. The domestic nature of the range was further emphasized by the addition of the north-east turret which was built primarily to house latrines serving each level of the building. Its external trefoil and quatrefoil windows confirm that defensibility cannot have been a high priority.

This reconstruction of the hall at Weobley provides an impression of the de la Bere family dining in the later fourteenth century (Illustration by Terry Ball, 1987).

THE KITCHEN

Retrace your steps to the basement area of the hall. Initially, this is believed to have served as both the hall and kitchen, and then in the second phase of the initial building period, when the hall was raised to first-floor level, it became the main kitchen for the castle. You will see that three wide windows lit the basement, and in the central splay there is a drain for waste. The windows were located low down on the face of the northern exterior curtain and consequently were barred with iron grilles and could be further secured by draw-bars for their shutters. Each was provided with a window seat offering comfortable views of the estuary — a luxury which may have originated with the early use of this chamber as a hall. The now mutilated kitchen fireplace was situated in the east wall of the basement chamber.

THE PORCH AND HALL BLOCK

Return to the courtyard, and then to the porch block, which was added by Sir Rhys ap Thomas in the late fifteenth century. It provided a more stately entrance to the hall and private quarters. The porch is entered through a tall archway of finely dressed stone, and inside, modern steps lead up to the lobby. From here, a late fifteenth-century doorway leads to a modern platform which stands at the level of the original wooden floor of the hall.

At the end of this platform a doorway enters a turret or watchtower which provided a look-out and gave access on to the wall-walk which circumnavigates the hall on three sides. The fourth or west wall is not of sufficient thickness to carry a wall-walk since it was never

intended to be an external wall, as indicated by the 'toothing' on the exterior of the hall wall seen at the beginning of the tour (p. 40).

Looking into the hall itself, the four corbels on the south wall, and the horizontal beam slots

The hall at Weobley was situated at first-floor level within the northern block. The recessed area of stonework behind the position of the high table may have been designed to house wooden panelling or tapestry hangings.

across the gables, mark the position of the original four-bay roof. The dais, or high table, would have been located at the far end of the hall. This was lit by a pair of opposing mullioned and transomed windows in the north and south walls, though the former was soon replaced by a fireplace. There is a third window of the same design in the east wall, which is the best surviving example in the hall.

The recess in the far wall was probably deliberately designed to house late-medieval wooden panelling or tapestry hangings. Such an overt decorative feature clearly demonstrates the domestic rather than the military role of Weobley at this time. This grand chamber would have been the focus of castle life in the fourteenth century and it is here that the family would have sat during meals, often entertaining neighbouring lords or visiting members of their kin.

Returning to the landing, the room beyond the lobby was much altered for a tenant farmer in the sixteenth century. The fireplace and corbelled out chimney belong to this period.

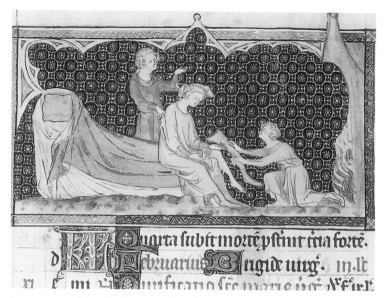

In common with medieval practice, the solar at Weobley was a well-appointed room to which the lord could retire in privacy and comfort. In this fourteenth-century manuscript illustration a man dresses in comfort within a private chamber (By kind permission of the British Library, Royal Ms. 2 B VIII, f. 72v).

THE SOLAR

Return to the basement of the hall and climb the modern wooden staircase to the solar, the lord's private chamber. This was a well-appointed room where the lord could retire in privacy and comfort. There was a fireplace with a large projecting hood, of which traces remain in the surrounding masonry, and three windows. The recesses housing the two larger mullioned and transomed windows contained side benches with views across Llanrhidian marsh to the north and the courtyard to the east.

A small doorway in the corner led, via a long mural passage, to a latrine. Part-way along this route there are rebates for a door to ensure privacy. Access to the room over the gateway could also be gained from this passage.

Finally, enter the deep basement under the solar which served as a cellar. The entrance is modern and appears to be cut through an enigmatic projecting structure which may have been constructed during the second period of building in the fifteenth century to provide direct access to the solar from the courtyard.

The cellar appears to have been much altered since it was originally constructed as a single chamber lit by three windows. The cross wall and stone vault date from the late fifteenth century.

Before leaving the castle, it is perhaps worth reflecting on its domestic character. The four ranges, despite their contracted form, each contained substantial and comfortable accommodation

for the de la Beres, their guests and retainers. Clearly, this was a household of some size and importance, reflecting the status and prominence of the family in the lordship of Gower.

A large mullioned and transomed window in the solar at Weobley looked out over the courtyard.

Begun about 1106, the only surviving upstanding masonry at Loughor Castle is a late thirteenth-century square tower.

A TOUR OF LOUGHOR CASTLE

Loughor Castle is carefully tucked within the corner of the Roman fort of *Leucarum*, overlooking a convenient crossing point of the river Llwchwr, on the main east–west route through south Wales. Begun by the Norman knight, Henry de Villiers, soon after 1106, only the earthwork defences of his stronghold survive today. During the next two hundred years the castle was gradually re-fortified in stone, culminating with the remaining stone tower which seems to have been constructed some time around the turn of the thirteenth century.

Today, the approach to the castle from the road is by way of a grassy landscaped slope which crosses the line of the curtain wall close to the stone tower. The position of the curtain wall is now marked by a low stony bank which almost completely encircles the level summit of the castle ringwork. Below this, skirting the foot of a steep scarp on the east and south sides, is a continuous terrace which marks the line of the ditch. The area enclosed is quite small and could have accommodated only limited storage and living facilities. Therefore it seems likely that an outer bailey or courtyard may have existed along the ridge towards the site of the church, in which additional accommodation would have been located.

The tower is the only upstanding masonry on the site and, although small, represents the most substantial structure to have existed here.

GROUND PLAN OF LOUGHOR CASTLE

N

Line of Roman Fort

Tower

Fallen Angle of Tower

Late Thirteenth or Early Fourteenth Century

0   5   10 Metres

0   10   20   30 Feet

A tripod pitcher of about 1200 found during excavations at Loughor Castle. It may have been manufactured in the Wiltshire area (By courtesy of the National Museum & Gallery, Cardiff).

As a residential building it would have been cramped, measuring just 23 feet by 26 feet (7m by 8m) externally, and consisting of a basement with two floors above, each containing a single chamber. Despite the provision of fireplaces and latrines the tower lacked any real comfort and would have seemed austere, for it was constructed entirely of Pennant sandstone slabs and devoid of any architectural decoration. The tower would have been roofed and may have had a battlement level though, unfortunately, insufficient masonry remains to guess at its appearance.

EXTERIOR OF THE TOWER

On entering the site the north wall of the tower faces you. Projecting from this wall of the tower is distinctive stone 'toothing'. These masonry 'teeth' would have been integrated into the curtain wall that was aligned with the side of the tower facing the courtyard. Following the outside walls of the tower, it is evident that it was built out over the ditch which has been partially filled in to provide stable foundations; the three outer walls of the tower were built at an angle — battered — for the same purpose. Although the lower courses of these walls have been robbed, the latrine chute which served both upper floors survives close to the south-west corner of the tower. On the south face itself can be seen further traces of the curtain above faint indications of a gate passage. This, together with evidence gleaned from the excavations (p. 6), suggests that the entrance to the castle has always been located in this position.

The large block of masonry lying in front of the tower consists of the south-east corner which contains the remains of the spiral stairs that would have given access to the two upper floors.

INTERIOR OF THE TOWER

The basement is entered through a wide door on the right of the courtyard side (east) of the tower. A second door near to the south-east corner gave access to the upper floors via the now collapsed mural stairs. Inside the main entrance can be seen

drawbar holes and a recess for the door to open into. Between the two doors was a narrow window which provided very limited light for the basement. It seems likely that this room was used for storage purposes since it could be barred from the inside and was perhaps accessible through a trap door from the first-floor room.

The floor of the chamber above was carried on seven large beams, the sockets for which can be clearly seen in the south wall. Access was directly from the courtyard via the collapsed stairs to a door on the south wall, one of whose sides is still visible. To the right of this is a latrine chamber lit by a tiny window.

The three remaining walls of the chamber each contain a window. Those to the more vulnerable west and north sides were barred with iron grilles and closed with wooden shutters. That on the courtyard side (east) is offset to the left of the wall to allow room for the now

disappeared door to the mural stairs. The room was heated by a plain, recessed fireplace in the north wall.

The upper floor was also reached via the collapsed mural stair. The arrangement in this chamber was almost identical to the room below with three windows, a latrine and a fireplace, this time in a rounded recess. The east window, however, was centrally placed, unlike its counterpart below, leaving no room for the collapsed stairs to have continued to battlement level. Had further stairs existed, they must have been located in the now vanished south wall.

To complete your visit, it is worth clambering down the steep grassy slope to the field on the south side of the site. The view back to the castle emphasizes its strategic position and thus why it rapidly became a symbol of control to both Norman and Welshman alike.

Left: Two of the original three storeys surviving in the single tower at Loughor. This view shows the entrance into the basement, with a plain fireplace set into the north wall of the first-floor apartment.

Right: An aerial view of Loughor Castle from the north-east. It was initially raised as an earth-and-timber 'ringwork' in the early twelfth century (Crown Copyright: The Royal Commission on the Ancient and Historical Monuments of Wales).

A TOUR OF SWANSEA CASTLE

Swansea Castle lies in the centre of the modern bustling city, partially hidden amongst the shops and office blocks which have been built in the vicinity. This should, perhaps, come as no surprise for the castle has always been surrounded by the paraphernalia of the contemporary townscape, as befitted its role as the *caput* or centre of the lordship of Gower.

Today, however, it is not easy to appreciate how the castle once dominated the borough, located high on a ridge above the river Tawe, occupying the southern portion of the inner defences of the earlier stone castle which lay to its north. Indeed, it was the third stronghold to be built in Swansea, lying some 55 yards (50m) south of the earth-and-timber fortification raised by Henry de Beaumont early in the twelfth century.

Much of what can be seen today was built in the late thirteenth or early fourteenth centuries, and consists of two blocks of buildings ranged around the southern and eastern sides of a courtyard. The greater part of this work is likely to have been instigated by the last two de Braose lords of Gower, William II (d. 1290) and William III (d. 1326), and their Mowbray descendant, John (d. 1361). But the castle's crowning glory is undoubtedly

A general view of the surviving remains of Swansea Castle. Much of what can be seen was probably raised in the late thirteenth or early fourteenth centuries, with the arcaded parapet probably added several decades later. It is difficult to appreciate the way the once far more extensive fortification would have dominated the medieval town.

GROUND AND FIRST FLOOR PLANS OF SWANSEA CASTLE

Mid Thirteenth Century

Late Thirteenth Century (1280)

Late Medieval

Modern and Uncertain

Note: The arcaded parapet of about 1340 does not feature in the plans at these levels.

0   5   10 Metres

0   10   20   30 Feet

Ground Floor   **First Floor**

the arcaded parapet, which was added to the external face of the south block, giving it an exotic yet uniform appearance. Although inspired by similar decoration at the episcopal palaces of St Davids and Lamphey, the builder cannot be identified with any certainty as Henry de Gower, bishop of St Davids (1328–47).

THE COURTYARD

Once inside the grassy courtyard, the quadrilateral plan of the castle is clear. The south and east sides are defined by the angled south block containing the solar and hall ranges, linked by a short stretch of curtain wall to the north-east

tower. Excavations have shown that a northern curtain wall extended westwards from this tower to a point close to Castle Bailey Street, along the line of which the western curtain wall and entrance were probably sited.

The modern level of the courtyard is over 3 feet (1m) higher than the original ground level, as demonstrated by the build-up of debris which now obscures the openings into the north-east tower and solar range. No traces have been recovered of the less substantial structures which may have been built against the curtain walls and may yet lie undiscovered beneath these accumulations.

The castle well, also located in the courtyard, was cleared of debris to a depth of 40 feet (12m).

SOUTH BLOCK
THE HALL RANGE

You should stand near the tree in the grassed courtyard area to observe the main features of the angled south block. It consists of two adjoining ranges, that to your right containing a first-floor hall, and that to the left, the solar. The two ranges were constructed at the same time, with the exception of the semi-circular stair tower, directly in front of you, which was added later, probably in the fourteenth century.

The remains of three doorways are visible at ground-floor level, one to the left of the stair tower (now blocked), and two to its right, one of which is now blocked. These doors opened into three separate vaulted chambers, each of which was lit by a tall cross oillet or arrowloop in the exterior (south) wall. To the far right, a blocked window can be seen which lit the room at this (west) end of the block. The east chamber was also lit from the courtyard side; but the window opening was broken through for a door into the stair tower.

Seen from this high vantage point, the arrangements of the hall and solar on the upper floor of Swansea Castle are better appreciated.

One of the tall cross oillets, or arrowloops, in the south wall of Swansea Castle.

There was no internal communication between the rooms, or with the hall, until the addition of the stair tower.

The hall and service rooms were located on the first floor. Remains of the arched entrance survive at this level to the right of the stair tower, and above it can be seen traces of a gabled porch which would have covered the external staircase from the courtyard. To the right of this door, a window indicates the location of the service rooms. These connected with the hall via three separate doorways in the intervening wall and were divided into two floors. There is likely to have been at least a buttery and pantry where food and drink would have been prepared for serving. A further room to the west may have been the kitchen.

Windows can be seen to either side of the stair tower, which, with pairs in the wall opposite, lit the hall. A further small, square opening on the south side, opposite the entrance, would presumably have lit the screens passage. The eastern or dais end of the hall was squared off by the insertion of a cross-wall (see plan) which created a small triangular chamber beyond, from where two doors gave access to the solar. The hall would have been the most important chamber in the castle, where formal business would have been conducted as well as entertainment for visiting dignitaries and loyal retainers.

The rooms in these buildings are not currently accessible, though it is possible to peer into the chambers below the hall and appreciate something of their structure.

SOUTH BLOCK
THE SOLAR RANGE

To the left of the hall block is the solar range which is set at an angle, over much more steeply sloping ground. As a result it has an extra basement level, built primarily to support the remaining two floors but useful for storage given its proximity to the river which formerly flowed much closer to the castle. Indeed, the only external entrance was through a postern door which is visible from outside the castle.

Facing you are doors set at various levels. The lower, which is now partially blocked by the level of material in the courtyard, gave access to one of two ground-floor chambers. This room was provided with a fireplace and latrine and was perhaps a guest chamber or the lodgings for an official, resident in the castle. A second, irregularly shaped room lay alongside it, but there was no access between the two chambers.

However, trapdoor access to this second room could be gained from the cellar below; a mural stair led to the solar above, thus enabling direct communication between all three floors.

The large doorway at first-floor level was the principal entrance to the solar.

This chamber would have provided both comfort and privacy for the lord and his family: there was a fireplace, seats in the recesses for the windows in the east wall, a discretely hidden latrine, and the hint of a vaulted gallery where musicians may have played or poets recited.

EAST CURTAIN

The east curtain extends for a short distance between the solar range and the north-east tower. Although it has been patched in places, the line is probably original, as is the masonry which underlies the corner of the north-east tower. Indeed, this is thought to be some of the earliest extant walling in the present castle. A blocked door at first-floor level of the tower gave access to the wall-walk along this curtain wall.

NORTH-EAST
TOWER

The north-east tower was formerly the debtor's prison, and was much altered for this use in the late eighteenth century until its closure in 1853. The tower is rectangular except for a stair projection at its north-west corner, the upper levels of which provide evidence for the line of the now demolished north curtain wall in the form of a blocked doorway. The similarity between the cross oillets in the tower and those in the south block suggests that the two buildings are close in date.

In this view of Swansea Castle from the north-west side, the solar block can be seen to the left and the hall block to the right.

The interior of the tower is no longer accessible; however, the ground floor is divided into three unequal vaulted chambers which, like the hall block, contained no means of internal communication with the floor above. The largest chamber occupied the south-west corner and was entered from a door at its west (left) end, located some depth below the present courtyard level. Only the head remains visible; it has been dated to the fifteenth century and is therefore a later insertion. To the right of this, part of a large window opening provides an opportunity to see into the chamber. In the far wall, a door provides access into the long thin chamber on the north side of the tower. The third room, in the south-east corner, was entered through a doorway from the courtyard. To the right of the door are the traces of a curved recess which may relate to a stair recorded at the beginning of the twentieth century. Two loops in the east wall (now blocked) lit the room.

The upper floor has been radically altered, principally when it was converted into four cells for use as a debtors' prison. These rooms were each provided with a fireplace and roofed with a double barrel vault of brick. The remains of two oillets can be seen in the north wall which, although now blocked, were enlarged into windows for the two cells on this side of the tower.

The prison presented strange contradictions for the debtor inmates — they were not provided with food or furniture unless they had the means to purchase such necessaries; yet they were allowed to bring the tools of their trade into the prison in order to earn money to pay off their debts. Indeed, in 1853, an inspector discovered that

'one of the debtors, a Swansea bookbinder, had brought in his presses and tools and was assisted by his two apprentices, the smaller of whom used to enter and leave the prison at will through a hole in the wall where the water-pump had once been located, and was permitted in his master's room by night'.

EXTERIOR OF THE CASTLE

To conclude your visit to Swansea Castle it is worth looking at the exterior of the buildings to appreciate their fine uniform appearance and prominent position above the former course of the river.

Cross the courtyard to the tall, slender latrine tower. Here, a small section of the earliest curtain wall is visible to the left of the tower which was added to the face of a pre-existing wall.

Tall pointed windows of the late thirteenth-century hall block were partially cut when the arcaded parapet was added about 1340.

This wall may belong to the initial enclosure of the site in stone between 1151 and 1215 (p. 8).

Continuing eastwards, the masonry becomes more regular, and the window arrangements for this side of the hall block can be observed. In particular, the arches above the two tall pointed windows have been partially cut away to accommodate the drip line of the arcaded parapet, demonstrating that this decorative architectural feature was a later addition. The sloping roof line of the hall is also visible at this point, between the arches of the parapet.

The parapet is Swansea's distinguishing feature and, as has been discussed (p. 19), suggests some sort of association with Henry de Gower. The arcade extends along the hall block and around the three sides of the solar block. Although a single arch continues onto the courtyard face of the solar it is unclear whether the arrangement existed any further along the interior face of these buildings.

Continuing towards the solar block, the ground drops away steeply towards the river and the necessity for its basement level and the postern door becomes obvious. A second basement door is modern.

Finally, the east curtain slopes up towards the north-east tower in which the various blocked arrowloops can be seen. From this point the strategic position of the castle can be best appreciated, as well as the extent of the alterations which it has undergone over some five hundred years. Yet despite the long recorded presence of the castle — or castles — the history of Swansea remains strangely enigmatic with few clues to the sequence of building which took place here.

All of the detailed dressed stonework in the rubble walls of Swansea Castle was carved from Sutton stone, quarried on the Glamorgan coast near Ogmore. This stone was probably left exposed and distinct from the otherwise rendered walls.

The Neolithic chambered tomb at Parc le Breos nestles in the Green Cwm valley at Parkmill. It was probably built sometime during the period 4000–3500 BC. It is not known how long the tomb remained in use (Skyscan Balloon Photography, for Cadw: Welsh Historic Monuments).

PARC LE BREOS
CHAMBERED TOMB

PREHISTORIC GOWER

This flint 'handaxe' found at Rhosili is the earliest known man-made object from Gower and dates from about 125,000 years ago (By permission of the National Museum & Gallery, Cardiff).

The Gower peninsula has played host to people from earliest times, attracting and adapting to waves of new settlers for over 125,000 years. The evidence for this changing flux of prehistoric occupants is often scant and varied, ranging from stray stone tools to massive stone-built burial chambers — all of which bear testimony to aspects of everyday life, ritual and death.

A single flint 'handaxe' from Rhosili is the earliest known man-made object from Gower and was perhaps lost or left by its owner some 125,000 years ago. It was not until nearly 100,000 years later that the sporadic presence of people on Gower is again recorded, principally from cave sites at Long Hole, Nottle Tor and Cathole.

The most famous, however, is Goat's Hole Cave, Paviland, where amongst a rich assemblage of tools and bones, the skeleton of the renowned 'Red Lady' was discovered by William Buckland in 1823. Subsequent study revealed that the bones were those of a young man, aged about twenty-five, who had been ceremonially buried about 30,000 years ago, just before the final advance of the last ice sheets. The body was buried with ivory bracelets and wands, and perforated sea-shells, all of which were enveloped with the ochre that had stained the bones red. Paviland must undoubtedly have been a site of some special significance at this time.

Some 15,000 years later, when the ice had begun to retreat and the climate improve, cave sites were again occupied. Evidence of transitory occupation by hunter-gatherer groups is attested by tools worked from flint and bone, at Cathole, and again, at Paviland.

Around 10,000 years ago, once the ice had finally disappeared and the sea-level begun to rise, the rich coastal fringes would have been attractive to the hunters, fishers and gatherers who now occupied Gower. Although the sea is likely to have still been some distance from the present coastline, evidence for this Mesolithic activity, in the form of stone-chipping floors, has been recovered from Burry Holms.

Life might have continued unabated in much the same way had not the revolutionary introduction of farming from continental Europe taken place, around 5,500 years ago, heralding the advent of the Neolithic. The introduction of domesticated plants and animals required the gradual clearance of woodland resulting in the wholesale transformation of the landscape; it also necessitated a more permanently settled way of life.

A reconstruction drawing of the burial of the 'Red Lady' at Goat's Hole Cave, Paviland. The young man was buried in this Gower cave some 30,000 years ago (By permission of the National Museum & Gallery, Cardiff).

NEOLITHIC BURIAL AND PARC LE BREOS

A composite reconstruction drawing which attempts to show several aspects of Neolithic burial practice in chambered tombs. A minimum of forty individuals are represented by the bones recovered from Parc le Breos. The bones in the chambers were moved around at some time, whereas the interments in the grave passage were secondary and later in date (Illustration by Tony Daly, by permission of the National Museum & Gallery, Cardiff).

Each of the chambers and the central passage at Parc le Braose contained the remains of several skeletons. It is difficult to be certain how many individuals were buried in the tomb, though the original estimate of twenty-four, made by Dr Morton Douglas in 1869, is too conservative. During the 1960–61 excavations, additional fragments of human bone were recovered from the floor of the tomb and recent re-examination of both collections has suggested that a minimum of forty individuals were buried in the tomb.

What is perhaps more interesting is the composition of the group and their disposition within the tomb. Of the forty individuals that were recorded, there was one infant and seven children; two were in excess of fifty and one individual was at least sixty years old. The remainder appear to have been men and women aged between twenty-five and forty years — one of whom was described as being of 'gigantic proportions'. Indeed, further evidence has suggested that the male population was tall and strongly built whilst the females were comparatively small and gracile. Such a population would be physically suited to a hunting way of life and it is perhaps no coincidence that chemical analysis of the bones has revealed that the Parc le Breos people had a diet rich in animal protein.

There does not seem to have been any age or sex discrimination affecting the grouping of the burials in each chamber and the passage. Any other form of differentiation would be almost impossible to recognize now and it may be that status or family group was a more significant determining factor. However, the condition of the bones within the chambers does suggest that the bodies were moved around at some time, unlike the bodies which were recovered from the passage area. Indeed, it seems likely that these interments were secondary and made at a later date than the main assemblages deposited in the chambers.

Little evidence survives reflecting the day-to-day aspects of Neolithic life other than a scattering of flint tools, sherds of pottery and animal bones. Occasionally, the foundations of a house or settlement have been identified, such as Clegyr Boia, near St Davids, in Pembrokeshire, but generally they are thought to have been too ephemeral to survive the rigours of time. Gower is apparently no exception in this respect.

In sharp contrast, however, is the survival of houses for the dead — massive stone-built tombs which still dominate the landscape. These 'megalithic' burial chambers were usually constructed of slabs or boulders set on end, covered by a massive capstone and hidden beneath a mound of earth or a stone cairn. It has been suggested that as people became more tied to the land so they developed tribal or kinship rights of territory and inheritance. The need for their validity to be affirmed was perhaps achieved through the overt presence of their ancestors, visually symbolized by the megalithic tombs, and made manifest by ritual ceremonies which seem to have taken place at the entrance to the chambers.

The construction of tombs required a great deal of effort and labour. Clearly, they must have been the result of collective enterprise, and would have represented monuments of great significance to the local community. Origins for the spread of the megalithic tradition have been sought all over the western seaboard of Europe, yet no firm explanation for their emergence has been forthcoming. What is clear, however, is that different ideas seem to have come from different directions, perhaps reflecting the complicated process of the movement of both people and ideas at this time. Indeed, Gower is well placed to receive sea-borne visitors and its easy accessibility may explain why more than one megalithic tradition appears to be present.

Arthur's Stone overlooks the whole of the Gower peninsula from its position on top of a false crest on Cefn Bryn. Although classed as a megalithic chambered tomb, there is some doubt as to whether it is in fact Neolithic at all.

MEGALITHIC TOMBS ON THE GOWER PENINSULA

Six megalithic chambered tombs survive on Gower. They can be divided into two groups based, in part, on geography, and, in part, on constructional similarity.

The western group is united principally by their situation on land generally less suited to agriculture; constructionally, the tombs display few similarities. The Sweyne's Howe are a pair of much ruined chambered tombs located high on Rhosili Down. Their cultural affinities are uncertain and comparisons have been drawn with chambered tombs in west Wales and Ireland.

Maen Ceti — better known as Arthur's Stone — is spectacularly sited on a false crest on Cefn Bryn. Its single massive capstone covers two chambers standing in the remains of a round cairn. It seems likely that the tomb was constructed by excavating beneath the capstone and inserting the uprights under it. Although classed with other megalithic chambered tombs on the Gower peninsula, there is some doubt about the age of Arthur's Stone and it may not be Neolithic at all.

The fourth tomb in this western group is situated on the eastern edge of Cefn Bryn, close to the village of Nicholaston. All that is now visible is a megalithic cist which was found to have been buried beneath a mound some 122 feet (37.2m) long, bounded by a rough stone kerb.

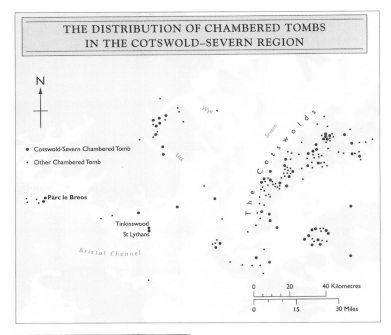

THE DISTRIBUTION OF CHAMBERED TOMBS
IN THE COTSWOLD–SEVERN REGION

N

• Cotswold-Severn Chambered Tomb
· Other Chambered Tomb

• Parc le Breos

Tinkinswood
St Lythans

Bristol Channel

0   20   40 Kilometres

0   15   30 Miles

with the bodies. However, sherds of pottery and animal bones have been recovered from the forecourt areas at some tombs and this has been interpreted as the debris from ritual feasting.

The partially exposed chambered tomb on Penmaen Burrows lies among sand dunes on a low headland flanking Three Cliffs Bay. Part of the entrance passage, the central chamber and the southern side chamber are still visible and it seems likely that a third chamber lay to the north. Although ruinous and denuded mainly of its cairn, this tomb reflects the Cotswold-Severn tradition. Like Parc le Breos, it can be classified by the transeptal arrangement of the chambers.

COTSWOLD-SEVERN CONNECTIONS

The south-eastern group consists of Parc le Breos and Penmaen Burrows and belongs to the so-called Cotswold-Severn tradition of megalithic construction. The term was first adopted by Glyn Daniel in 1937 when describing the group of tombs which extend over a considerable area bordering the upper reaches of the Severn estuary, extending as far as central Wessex.

The group is distinguished by their trapezoidal — or wedge-shaped — cairns, with pronounced forecourts and revetted by drystone walling. Within this overall plan, three different chamber forms further categorize the group. The simplest are those tombs with a single chamber entered directly from the forecourt, such as Tinkinswood and St Lythans, Vale of Glamorgan.

More elaborate are those with several chambers or transepts opening from a passage leading from the forecourt entrance, as at Parc le Breos. The third permutation consists of a 'blind entrance' in the forecourt with the chambers located and entered from the lateral sides of the cairn. The fully excavated tomb at Gwernvale, Powys, displays this form of construction.

There has been much debate concerning the chronology of the three types of chamber arrangement as well as discussion about the disposition of skeletal material within them. Some of the tombs appear to have been in use for a very long time, during which repeated burials sometimes led to the removal of previously interred bodies to different parts of the tomb. Moreover, corpses may have been excarnated — left to decompose — prior to burial, which may also account for the sometimes seemingly disorganized arrangement of bones within the chambers.

Rarely have grave goods of any description been found buried

PARC LE BREOS INVESTIGATED

Parc le Breos — the Giant's Grave — nestles in a grassy crook of the Green Cwm valley, cradled on either side by steeply wooded limestone cliffs. Today, the site is approached via a footpath along the now dry valley floor and its low, unassuming appearance belies the remarkable achievement which this massive megalithic tomb represents.

To the builders of the tomb, however, the valley probably looked quite different. It seems likely that a stream flowed close to the site at this time and that damp scrubby woodland had invaded the valley floor. Just 270 yards (250m) further up the valley is Cathole Cave, a natural rock shelter which has produced archaeological evidence from the Upper Palaeolithic, Mesolithic and Bronze Age periods indicating a long-standing human interest in the locality; moreover, the very presence of the cave may have influenced the unusual siting of the Neolithic tomb.

Radiocarbon dating of bones from the tomb has yielded a range of dates from around 3,800 to 3,000 B.C. It therefore seems likely that Parc le Breos was built sometime during the first half of the fourth millennium B.C. It is not known for how long the tomb was in use, but given the range of dates, it may have been for a number of centuries. When the chambers were finally closed, the forecourt and entrance appear to have been deliberately blocked with stone rubble infill.

The site appears not to have attracted antiquarian attention until 1869 when the owner, Henry Hussey Vivian (later Lord Swansea) was informed of the presence of skeletons by workmen stripping the stones of the cairn for use in road construction. His friend, and fellow antiquary, Sir John Lubbock, partially explored the site, reporting the results of the excavations in the London *Journal of the Ethnological Society*, accompanied by a report on the skeletons by Dr D. M. Douglas. Following this work, the skeletons were reinterred in the chambers and passage of the tomb, buried inside fire-clay retorts from the spelter works at Swansea, owned by the Vivian family.

However, it was not until 1937 when Daniel re-excavated the tomb that the elongated shape and form of the structure were recognized. Parc le Breos was further excavated by Richard Atkinson in 1960–61, when the tomb was cleared of trees, fully consolidated, and laid out for display.

The tomb at Parc le Breos was first investigated in 1869, though its true form and design was not recognized until further excavations in 1937 and 1960–61.

A DESCRIPTION OF THE TOMB

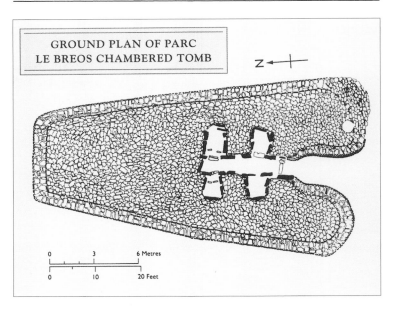

GROUND PLAN OF PARC
LE BREOS CHAMBERED TOMB

Parc le Breos lies on a north-east axis along the length of the valley so that the burial chamber is approached from its original entrance to the south.

It is immediately apparent that the tomb has been heavily restored though the cairn has not been replaced to the full height of the chambers, for there is no evidence to suppose that this would have been the original arrangement. The cairn itself is wedge shaped, some 72 feet (22m) long with a maximum width of about 40 feet (12m) at the southern end, tapering to just 20 feet (6m) at the north. It is built of coarse limestone slabs, pitched at random, which even today are easily obtainable from the valley sides.

The cairn is revetted with a drystone wall built of regularly coursed limestone slabs with occasional diagonal courses. The height (2 feet — 60cm) of this outer wall was determined from the collapsed debris found during the 1960–61 excavations. Excavation also revealed the existence of a second wall running parallel some 2 1/2 feet (75cm) behind the outer face. But unlike the outer wall, the inner revetment stopped just short of the northern end of the cairn. This wall, too, was intended as a revetment to resist the lateral thrust of the cairn material. However, this inner revetment was never intended to be seen (indeed, today it is covered by the cairn material) and consequently was built of coarse rubble blocks. The gap between these two walls was filled with flat limestone blocks laid more or less horizontally.

On the eastern side of the cairn, below the drystone wall, there are rounded iron-stained boulders, particularly in the area adjacent to the eastern horn of the forecourt which is now partially collapsed. It has been suggested that this collapse and erosion were caused by the former presence of the stream. Alternatively, these boulders may be the remnants of an earlier feature on the site. A number of the brown-coloured, iron-stained boulders which were recovered from the collapsed wall have been placed on the edge of the cairn.

The deep forecourt entrance to the tomb led into a central passage, with two pairs of side or transeptal chambers. The internal divisions may represent symbolic demarcation of space, perhaps related to the status of individual burials.

If this replicates their original position, the contrast of the brown with the grey angular cairn material would have been visually quite striking.

The tomb was entered via a deep forecourt, with S-shaped revetment walls, at the south end of the cairn. On excavation the forecourt was found to have been deliberately blocked with stones. From beneath this blocking, on the old ground surface, fragments of human bone, calcite and pottery sherds were recovered. Although sparse, this evidence of activity may reflect something of the ritual that has been recognized at other Cotswold-Severn burial chambers.

The burial area itself comprises two pairs of side, or transeptal, chambers opening off a central passage. All are constructed using limestone slabs, with the intervening gaps filled with dry-stone walling.

The eastern jamb of the entrance was missing and has been replaced with a modern replica from a quarry at nearby Ilston. Sill stones mark the thresholds to the passage and to three of the chambers, and it seems likely that the fourth has simply gone missing through time. The two northern chambers also have further sill stones inside the chambers dividing each of them unequally into two distinct areas. Archaeologists believe that such divisions may be a symbolic demarcation of space, reflecting distinctions among the burials within the differently designated areas.

Although the roofing arrangements have disappeared, there are likely to have been several overlapping courses of slabs forming a corbel on to which a capstone, or further corbelling, would have been placed.

FURTHER READING

Acknowledgement

The author and Cadw would like to thank the Royal Commission on the Ancient and Historical Monuments of Wales for permission to draw on its forthcoming material on the castles at Swansea and Weobley. In addition, Professor Alasdair Whittle and Mr M. Wysocki have made available details of a forthcoming report on Parc le Breos. Dr F. G. Cowley, Professor R. R. Davies and Professor Sir Glanmor Williams have made significant contributions to the content of the guidebook.

General Works

David Crouch, 'Oddities in the Early History of the Marcher Lordship of Gower, 1107–1166', *Bulletin of the Board of Celtic Studies*, **31** (1984), 133–42.

J. D. Davies, *A History of West Gower*, 4 volumes (Swansea 1877–94).

R. R. Davies, *Conquest, Coexistence and Change: Wales 1063–1415* (Oxford 1987); reprinted in paperback as, *The Age of Conquest: Wales 1063–1415* (Oxford 1991).

W. H. Jones, *History of Swansea and the Lordship of Gower* (Carmarthen 1920).

T. B. Pugh, editor, *Glamorgan County History, Volume III: The Middle Ages* (Cardiff 1971)

The Royal Commission on Ancient and Historical Monuments in Wales, *An Inventory of the Ancient Monuments in Glamorgan, Volume III, Part Ia: The Early Castles* (London 1991).

H. N. Savory, editor, *Glamorgan County History Volume II: Early Glamorgan, Pre-history and Early History* (Cardiff 1984).

Glanmor Williams, editor, *Glamorgan County History, Volume IV: Early Modern Glamorgan* (Cardiff 1974).

Glanmor Williams, *Recovery Reorientation and Reformation: Wales c. 1415–1642* (Oxford 1987); reprinted in paperback as, *Renewal and Reformation: Wales c. 1415–1642* (Oxford 1993).

Oxwich Castle

J. M. Lewis, 'The Oxwich Brooch', *Jewellery Studies*, **2** (1985), 23–29.

Bernard Morris, 'Oxwich Castle', *Gower*, **25** (1974), 1–15.

Bernard Morris, 'Oxwich Castle: Which Came First, the Farmhouse or the Hall?', *Gower*, **43** (1992), 42–47.

The Royal Commission on Ancient and Historical Monuments in Wales, *An Inventory of the Ancient Monuments in Glamorgan, Volume IV, Part I: The Greater Houses* (London 1981), 63–76.

Glanmor Williams, 'Rice Mansell of Oxwich and Margam (1487–1559)', *Morgannwg*, **6** (1962), 33–51.

Glanmor Williams, 'The Herberts, the Mansells and Oxwich Castle', in John R. Kenyon and Richard Avent, editors, *Castles in Wales and the Marches* (Cardiff 1987), 173–83.

Weobley Castle

W. G. Thomas, *Weobley Castle* (HMSO, London 1971).

Loughor Castle

J. M. Lewis, 'Excavations at Loughor Castle, West Glamorgan 1969–73', *Archaeologia Cambrensis*, **142** (1993), 99–181.

Swansea Castle

Bernard Morris, *Swansea Castle* (Swansea 1992)

C. J. Spurgeon, 'Swansea Castle — The Surviving Remains', in Edith Evans, *Swansea Castle and the Medieval Town* (Swansea 1983), 27–35

Parc Le Breos Chambered Tomb

G. E. Daniel, 'The Chambered Barrow in Parc le Breos Cwm, S. Wales', *Proceedings of the Prehistoric Society*, **3** (1937), 71–86.

The Royal Commission on Ancient and Historical Monuments in Wales, *An Inventory of the Ancient Monuments in Glamorgan, Volume I: Pre-Norman, Part I: The Stone and Bronze Ages* (London 1976), 34–5.

Sir John Lubbock, 'Description of the Parc Cwm Tumulus', *Journal of the Ethnological Society*, new series, **2** (1871); reprinted in, *Archaeologia Cambrensis*, fourth series, **2** (1871), 168–72.

Sian Rees, *Parc le Breos Chambered Tomb* (Cardiff 1980)